ALA Editions • **SPECIAL REPORTS**

GRASSROOTS LIBRARY ADVOCACY

LAUREN COMITO
ALIQAE GERACI
CHRISTIAN ZABRISKIE

AMERICAN LIBRARY ASSOCIATION
Chicago 2012

Lauren Comito is an outreach librarian at Queens Library. She is a passionate advocate for library services in New York City and elsewhere. She works as the webmaster and managing editor for the website savenyclibraries.org and as the communications director for Urban Librarians Unite and the Save NYC Libraries campaign. Lauren earned her master's degree in library science at Queens College and a BFA in Studio Art at Brooklyn College.

Aliqae Geraci is an industrial and labor relations research librarian at Catherwood Library, Cornell University, and a former public librarian. She is a founding member of Urban Librarians Unite and the Save NYC Libraries campaign, and she writes and speaks on topics related to labor, independent publishing, and radical librarianship. Aliqae has an MSLIS from Long Island University and an MA in labor studies from the City University of New York.

Christian Zabriskie is the assistant coordinator of young-adult services for Queens Library. He is the founder of Urban Librarians Unite and the Save NYC Libraries campaign. He also writes and speaks about graphic novels in libraries and topics in young adult library services. Christian has an MA in English language and literature from the University of St. Andrews in Scotland and an MSLIS from Florida State University.

© 2012 by the American Library Association. Any claim of copyright is subject to applicable limitations and exceptions, such as rights of fair use and library copying pursuant to Sections 107 and 108 of the U.S. Copyright Act. No copyright is claimed in content that is in the public domain, such as works of the U.S. government.

Printed in the United States of America

16 15 14 13 12   5 4 3 2 1

Extensive effort has gone into ensuring the reliability of the information in this book; however, the publisher makes no warranty, express or implied, with respect to the material contained herein.

ISBNs: 978-0-8389-1134-1 (paper); 978-0-8389-9499-3 (PDF); 978-0-8389-9498-6 (ePub); 978-0-8389-9500-6 (Kindle). For more information on digital formats, visit the ALA Store at alastore.ala.org and select eEditions.

Library of Congress Cataloging-in-Publication Data
Comito, Lauren.
　　　Grassroots library advocacy : a special report / Lauren Comito, Aliqae Geraci, Christian Zabriskie.
　　　　　pages　　　cm
　　　Includes bibliographical references and index.
　　　ISBN 978-0-8389-1134-1 (alk. paper)
　　　　1. Libraries—Public relations—United States. 2. Libraries and community—United States. 3. Library outreach programs—United States. 4. Libraries—Political aspects—United States. 5. Pressure groups—United States. 6. Community organization—United States. I. Geraci, Aliqae. II. Zabriskie, Christian. III. Title.
　　　Z716.3.C66 2012
　　　021.70973—dc23　　　　　　　　　　　　　　　　　　　2012016969

Series cover design by Casey Bayer.
Series text design in Palatino Linotype and Avenir by Karen Sheets de Gracia.

♾ This paper meets the requirements of ANSI/NISO Z39.48-1992 (Permanence of Paper).

To David Grimes, my Library Dad — LC

To all the Library Warriors — AG

To Vicky, the heart of my everything — CZ

CONTENTS

WEB Editable versions of the appendix materials are
available at **www.alaeditions.org/webextras/**.

INTRODUCTION

The weather at the 24-Hour Read-In was bad from the outset. We set up in the rain, and a steady drizzle continued from when the first reader stepped up to the microphone. We had two small overhead tents, one for the reader and one with space for about eight or nine chairs packed tightly. The rain tapered off just in time for our VIPs, but as the sun went down, it picked up again, and the temperature started to drop. Early June in New York City can be changeable, and when the wind increased, everyone bundled up. By 2:00 a.m. the rain was lashing, and the wind was strong enough to shake and twist the tents. Readers had to avoid the trickle of water just short of the podium, and the listeners were shivering even though they were wrapped in blankets.

Why did we do it? To focus attention on the importance of libraries and to raise public awareness of a proposed budget cut that would have been devastating. For twenty-four hours hundreds of readers raised their voices in fifteen-minute shifts on the steps of the Brooklyn Public Library. We read and listened in turn; the listeners acted as witnesses and as a visible symbol of the general public. The amazing thing was that no matter the time or the weather, there were always people sitting, listening, and eager to stand up and read. We are not alone. During the past few years, library supporters from all over the world have stood up to defend their library and what it means to their community. Libraries are increasingly under fire, and in response, people in California, in Britain, in New York City, and all over the map are creatively speaking out in large and small ways about their quietest public institution.

Libraries, like many other public service providers in the United States, have been the victim of increasing budget cuts in the wake of the 2008 economic crisis. Declining tax revenue and the increasing popularity of political belief systems that challenge government services have fueled these cuts. A recent study published in *Library Journal* stated that more than 72 percent of public libraries surveyed had been the target of budget cuts in the previous year, with 43 percent of respondents reporting staff layoffs.[1] Library budget cuts have an immediately devastating impact on service and staffing levels, endangering public access to essential information and community resources.

Yet despite declining funding and service levels, public library use is up and continues to grow. A recent telephone survey of American households by the American Library Association found that households reporting more than twenty public library visits in a year rose to 25.4 million in 2009 from 20.3 million in 2006.[2] Increases to the user base can be attributed to patrons flocking to their libraries to receive job search assistance, access the Internet, and take advantage of free education and entertainment. This growing demand for service in the face of declining tax revenues places municipalities in the unenviable position of having to slash funding even to popular and beloved services. In addition, given the choice between closures and layoffs, many systems have reduced staff when they are needed most.

Of course, library advocacy is most visible during budget time; lack of funds is axiomatic to our profession. Libraries always have to speak up to get their slice of the budget pie, and they have done so quite well for many years. As budgets tighten, however, the slices become thinner, verging on starvation rations. Libraries must ask more loudly and more often for what they need, and incredulous library professionals are left to wonder about extension of the modest benefits that have taken them years to accrue.

However, jobs and benefits are only part of the equation. There's also the issue of having the operational capacity to fulfill responsibilities to the public. The library has a unique place in society. It is a cultural storehouse for the community it serves, whatever that community may be. It offers dignity and sanctuary to everyone. It is the leveling ground where millionaires and migrants meet, often with much the same needs. It is the poor man's university, a community for the friendless, and a repository of both knowledge and opportunity for all. As an educational institution, in service to the people, the library, a space dedicated to freely accessible information and entertainment presented in a welcoming, supportive atmosphere, is an idea worth defending. It is a courageous concept, a bold statement about the priorities of our culture: a great many very talented people have made moving this idea forward their life's work. Thanks to their efforts, libraries are endemic in our communities. This did not happen overnight, nor will the dismantling of our libraries be immediate. But libraries are being pared back, hampered by new budget "realities" that move them to the bottom of the list of public priorities. They are low-hanging fruit for budget trimmings, even when their budgets have already been carved to the bone. A steady chipping away of staff, service, hours, and access points continuing over years and decades threatens the existence of public libraries as a reliable community resource. The process has already begun, and stemming the tide requires relentless effort from passionate library defenders.

You can organize within your community to save the library that has served you so well for so long. We hope this book will help you. Libraries' most valuable sources of talent and creativity are the workers who staff them and the patrons who use them. The ideas presented here aim to harness that talent and energy and direct it toward advocating for public library support and funding. Throughout our book we make a key distinction between expressing support and being an effective advocate. Just telling everyone how great the library is, even shouting it from the rooftops, is not enough. To change your library's political and economic reality, words must be coupled with active, targeted campaigning. Libraries must come to be viewed as the last place anyone wants to cut because of the resultant political fallout.

You don't need a lot of people or money to make an impact; you just need a clear direction and some guidance to become a library activist leader. Our organization, Urban Librarians Unite, started out with a completely different mission. We began as a way to encourage conversation among librarians working in the three massive public library systems in New York City (Brooklyn Public Library, New York Public Library, and Queens Library), but we quickly expanded the conversation to include the broader library community in the city. After two years of monthly meetings, we had several hundred very loosely connected members. It was a fun group with a very simple mandate: meet once a month to swap ideas, vent, and have a few laughs.

Then the economy went sour, and budget cuts loomed huge for New York City's public libraries. The city's proposed cuts for 2011 would have closed dozens of libraries, put hundreds of librarians out of work, decimated our membership. Within two weeks of deciding to retool into an activist organization, we had a postcard campaign up and running. When we first started organizing as ULU, we came from a wide range of experience and comfort with political activism. Some of us were well versed in working in activist channels and pressure campaigns; some of us had formal experience working within government or nonprofits; some knew little, if anything, about activism. But we had two things in common: we were all library workers, used to navigating the complex and rapidly changing landscape of New York City, and we were decidedly done with accepting a status quo that had resulted in massive cuts to public library services in our systems. Seeing hundreds of pink slips go out to dedicated public servants was the last straw for us. So we organized, and we started to shout out, "We will not be shushed!" In a fit of inspiration Lauren created our logo, which she silk-screened by hand onto hundreds of T-shirts, and our fight began in earnest. By the end of that month we were organizing the 24-Hour Read-In on the steps of Brooklyn Public Library. Our tiny organization's big event was covered by the *New York Times*; the *Wall Street Journal*; the BBC; PBS; and numerous local television, radio, and print media. There were still cuts that year, but much fewer than threatened. When the budget dance started up again the following year, we were ready to go, with the luxury of experience and a longer lead time. We made mistakes; that's part of the process. But they never stopped us from going forward, and they shouldn't stop you.

Through it all we have stayed tiny and broke. It took four years of meetings before we even considered looking into incorporation. We never had a budget or a treasurer, because there was never any money. That's changed, but not by much. A handful of dedicated volunteers still form the nucleus of the group, but their efforts pull off massive events that bring in hundreds of people. We know you don't need a lot of money or a horde of volunteers. What you need is creativity, dedication, and a group willing to work very hard.

This book comes out of the lessons that we learned along the way. The basics are here: how to organize; the importance of communication; thinking strategically; and most important, getting active. There is a great emphasis on Web 2.0 tools because they have been absolutely crucial to our efforts. Message is vital, but so is delivery, and there have never been as many options for getting your ideas out there as there are today. Those tools need to be coupled with real-life action, so we emphasize boots-on-the-ground activism as well.

Some of the suggestions we provide here might cause people to tell you you're nuts. That's kind of the point! Society and the media have evolved in such a way that the only means to bring attention to a cause, no matter how worthy, is to be a little bit different. We like to call this the calculated crazy. As an activist, you aren't trying to get press attention just for the sake of getting in the paper; you have a purpose. That purpose should color and drive all your actions. Once you've done your crazy thing, and have the attention you need, remember your message and lay out the issues in a clear, concise way. That's how you capitalize on your unique event or action. As professionals, librarians have a reputation for being quiet and meek. You can use the dichotomy between that reputation and your very loud reality to make a huge impact on your community and your library. We'll show you how to do that.

This brief book is intended as a primer to help you get going. Activism is exciting stuff. Your hard work can make a visible difference in your community. You will encounter a lot of things that are not in this book. That is the nature of the work. Every community is different, every library is different, and every campaign is different. Try out things, see how they work, then go back to the drawing board for improvements. You'll learn something every time you do something. Make the next campaign stronger, and the one after that event bigger. Take note of what went well and duplicate it; take note of what went poorly and eliminate it. If an event tanks, roll with the punches, and make your next endeavor totally different. If you have an event that is a roaring success, use it as a springboard to build momentum for your next action.

Stay engaged. Don't let naysayers slow you down. Don't let the glacial rate of progress exhaust you. Don't let setbacks define who you are. Sometimes it feels like you are alone, shouting in a scary woods. We say, "Shout anyway! Shout until your throat is bloody! Shout until every wolf in the forest hears you!" At least you will know that in the end you did everything you could for what you believed in.

Let's not play around here. The library is an institution of equality and dignity. It is a community meeting ground, the common third space, a titanium crowbar that can leverage people up out of challenging situations. Hyperbole you say? Your critics certainly will. They will bring out all the old and crusty arguments: "Libraries do a little here, a little there; they check out John Grisham novels, and give homeless guys a place to sleep—so what?"

We disagree with the naysayers. For us the library is almost a sacred space. It is a trust, a duty, a calling. We deal in potential, in hope, in knowledge. We offer dreams, progress, solace, laughter. Where else in your community is a beggar treated the same as a doctor? Where else can a child trump a rich guy in a suit? Where else can a big thinker explore everything that there is to know in the world—all for free?

That is what you are fighting for. You are fighting for those ineffable moments when the library is the *only* resource that a person can turn to. You are fighting for the people who are hidden in the cracks and sit on the fringes. You are a warrior for children's imaginations and for everyone's right to their share of culture, learning, and entertainment. It is not an easy thing to fight for sometimes; you should know that now. There are times when the ideas elude the imagination of the people you are trying to convince. Sometimes there are so many other concerns it is almost impossible to make your voice heard amid the chatter. And there are times when just keeping your movement together feels like clutching sand in your fist.

Take heart. What you do is worth it. What you do, you do for future generations. What you do, you do for the cultural heritage of your community. What you do will continue to change lives, quietly—like the library itself.

NOTES

1. Michael Kelley, "LJ's 2010 Budget Survey: Bottoming Out?" January 15, 2011, www.libraryjournal.com/lj/ljinprintcurrentissue/888434-403/bottomingout.html.csp.

2. Denise M. Davis, *The Condition of U.S. Libraries: Public Library Trends, 2002–2009.* American Library Association Office for Research and Statistics, 2009. www.ala .org/research/sites/ala.org.research/files/content/librarystats/public/Condition_of _Libraries_1999.20.pdf.

1

GETTING STARTED

No one wants to go into a fight blindfolded, so before embarking on a library advocacy campaign, it is important for you and your group to consider a few basic issues. You need to decide which methods of persuasion you will use; who you should be talking to; and most important, what your group's mission and goals will be. Thinking about these key issues at the very beginning will let you avoid unnecessary blunders and will bring you a long way toward implementing a successful campaign for public libraries in your community.

Knowing what you want to get from your efforts is the key. You must have a clearly defined goal. Are you facing a particularly bad budget year? Are you floating a bond for a new building? Is the library contemplating closures and layoffs? Once you have identified your target issue and what you are advocating for, you can begin to delineate the parameters of your fight.

Who do you need to influence in order to achieve your goal? Who holds the power in your community? Is your library's budget linked to another city agency, such as the school system? Asking these questions in the beginning will save you time in the end. There is no point in lobbying the city council (e.g., selectmen, aldermen, board) if the mayor, and only the mayor, writes the budget. Once you have identified the funding structure and the decision makers who hold the reins of power, your group can put together a strategy.

Building public awareness is an essential part of your mission, regardless of your city's political landscape. In some cases, such as a ballot referendum on funding, the public will be your primary target audience. Even when you are not trying to influence a public vote, increasing the public's awareness and gaining its sympathy remain vital. Politicians are keenly aware of public perceptions and the pulse of the community, and public opinion will exert far more pressure on elected officials than your organization could ever hope to do on its own. Steadily building public pressure by way of press coverage, event attendance, and successful petition and postcard- or letter-writing campaigns will be a major motivating force for elected officials to take action on your issue. If you can successfully make your cause a popular public issue, your battle will be half won.

At the same time, you must know where and when to focus public attention. Leading a public hue and cry against a mayor who has no control over the budget or a bond will do nothing to help your cause—and will possibly alienate a potential supporter, predisposing him or her against the library the next time an issue comes up. Do your research, and determine where your leverage points are.

Part of understanding the power players is being aware of their schedules. When are your city's budget talks? How far in advance of those formal discussions is the budget on people's radar? How long can you realistically keep your loosely affiliated activist group working together, and when should you try to have enthusiasm and activism peak? Having an August read-in in support of the library budget may harm your cause more than help it if the budget won't be discussed until the following April. When budget talks finally roll around eight months later, the only thing remaining from that day of passionate advocacy will be a bunch of old photos on your website. Pictures of people in shorts do little to help your cause when there is still snow on the ground.

It is important to identify key dates and elections so you can target your efforts accordingly. Plan your events and solicit media coverage to attract the most attention. Don't be afraid to connect library issues to what's going on in the broader political landscape, such as an election in which a library advocate or opponent is in a fight for office. Do not underestimate the importance of timing. Timing is crucial.

We learned that the hard way. Our advocacy group, Urban Librarians Unite, organized a zombie walk over Brooklyn Bridge to New York City Hall on Halloween to protest pending budget cuts. We thought we covered all our bases. We sent out press releases; got our permits; notified key allies; and had great attendance, with more than fifty undead librarians in full costume and makeup lurching across the bridge on a beautiful day. Tons of press came out and took a bunch of pictures and conducted interviews. But nobody ran a single story. Unfortunately, we made the mistake of holding the march on the Sunday before a hotly contested midterm election on Tuesday. Our timing was off by forty-eight hours. There was absolutely no way our march was going to make it into the papers; at any other time it would have been a lock. It was an odd (and rather painful) lesson in how important timing can be.

> Urban Librarians Unite was originally designed as a social and professional group dedicated to bringing librarians from around the city together and fostering communication among professionals from different disciplines and among the three major library systems, whose more than two hundred branches provide service to New York City. It successfully operated as a monthly drinks, idea swap, and gripe session for about two years. When a library budget crisis hit and many of our members were at risk of losing their jobs, we quickly retooled into an activist organization. The structure and communications were already in place, so it was relatively easy to give members a direction, fire them up, and get them moving to protest the budget cuts.

IDENTIFYING PROFESSIONAL AND ORGANIZATIONAL LIMITATIONS

All citizens have the right to free speech, but members of your group may be bound by outside considerations that have an impact on what they can do to help. For instance, library employees may be limited by what they can do on the library's time or prohibited from speaking to the press about library issues. Some public-sector workplaces prohibit all outside political activity. You should absolutely check your local ordinances and relevant work regulations to identify what your municipality, administration, and board of trustees view as permissible activity before you plan a strategy that includes events, protests, or canvassing campaigns. In this way you can protect your members and ensure their greatest participation. All this may sound like a pain, but it is important. Ask the union, human resources, and pretty much everybody you can think of to make sure what you and your supporters can and cannot do. Nobody should get fired because they were part of your rally.

Advocating in the library may be easier than you expect, and some state and local governments and library administrations are more tolerant than others. In New York City, where the library systems are private nonprofits, library staff were encouraged to put out petitions and postcards at our reference desks, given excused time to rally at city hall, and allowed to hold demonstrations outside of library buildings. We were very fortunate that the library boards were supportive and encouraging of our efforts and that local ordinances did not prevent us from physically advocating for our cause. We must give credit where credit is due: despite an uphill battle for public opinion, we had the benefit of political and institutional support. This support helped our cause while adding creative allies who could be a little more "out there" than traditional library advocates, such as friends-of-the-libraries groups and the libraries themselves.

Activists in other cities and states may have limitations even if the advocacy campaign is independent of the library, the friends-of-the-library group, and the public-service union. If your board of trustees feels that it is inappropriate to have political petitions at the desk or if legislation prohibits it, then that is that. Don't fight. Figure out a way around the problem. Use it as an opportunity to directly engage potential supporters outside of the library. Library administration and local governments (more than likely) can't stop you from following the same parameters as other petition drives located in front of the library. Find out exactly what your local rules are for soliciting signatures in the park or in the mall, and follow them to the letter. Do not use obstacles and limitations as excuses to avoid outreach efforts. If your are stymied in your efforts to gather displays of support in public places, then explore private options like a church group, a college campus, or a service club. Are your tactics garnering pressure against your campaign? Consider making the opposition's platform part of your narrative, but be aware that doing so may galvanize any opponents you already have.

Library workers can use the advocacy campaign as an opportunity to gain additional supporters within the library, but don't let your efforts negatively affect the quality of service you provide to the public. If anything, advocacy should inspire you to give better service than ever before (see the section "Constant Advocacy" in chapter 3). In serving the public, you serve all of the public—including the guy who is trying to get your Carnegie library torn down to build a parking lot. When your bitterest opponent needs a book, he or she should absolutely receive the same service and anonymity as your most fervent supporter. This approach may well turn your opponents into allies.

ORGANIZATIONAL IDENTITY

What kind of group do you want to be? This question may be unexpectedly difficult to answer. An open-ended goal statement such as "We want to raise awareness of the library" is serviceable, but it is a better fit for long-standing traditional organizations like a local friends-of-the-library group. Open-ended, long-term goals are fine for ongoing charitable work or for a service club, but it is difficult to maintain an active grassroots advocacy effort without a specific goal in mind. Motivation is a key issue in an advocacy campaign. It is much easier to excite members and supporters if you are able to communicate goals and identify concrete successes.

It is important that your group define itself in the beginning. You don't have to wait until you have twenty people in the room before you lay out your basic mission, name, and purpose. Just go for it! Figuring out your organizational identity will allow you to more efficiently pursue your group's defining purpose and stay focused on that goal. It's easy to get lost in the minutiae of events and press releases before really discussing the internal aspects of your organization. That is why it is important that you determine what you are about early on. Having a clear message, goal, and identity will make it easier for you to formulate press releases and organize people for events in the thick of

THE WHY AND HOW OF TACTICAL THINKING

Tactical thinking is simply being careful with your resources and using them to best effect. It means knowing where best to put pressure, when best to apply it, and who in your organization is best suited to the task at hand. As the term implies, tactical thinking invites a more aggressive kind of activism. It means looking at the campaign, if not as a war, then at least as a game to be won through intelligent perseverance. A large part of tactical thinking is assessing your opponent and yourself. Where are your opponents stronger than you? In what area are your opponents' sources greater than yours, and to what ends are they dedicating those resources? Where are they slow to respond, and how can you use the issues in their message to your best advantage? If the opposition is strong in a given area—if it has the mass of the public or politicians locked up on their side—then avoid confrontation in that area. Focus on the mayor, or the budget office, or the press, or the public opinion and have those people influence the town council for you. If you have a particular strength, embrace it. Are a lot of college students or mommy groups on your side? Create opportunities for these populations to come to the forefront, and design events that will use them to best effect.

Tactical thinking means knowing your own weaknesses and avoiding confrontations in those areas. It means knowing your opponents' weaknesses and leaning on them. Tactical thinking should be an ongoing assessment of your organization and the problem(s) it intends to tackle. This does imply a more dynamic (if not aggressive) activism, the level of which is up to each campaign and its leadership. Tactical thinking is a means of organizational growth and efficiency. It helps leadership be aware of organizational assets and allows them to use those assets for the greatest impact.

the campaign. By identifying your direction early on, your supporters will find it easier to join and share in a larger vision as you build momentum and organizational strength.

Once you have identified your political landscape and organizational goals, you can focus on the internal issues of organizational structure. Don't bypass this step! Your group's structure and methods of organizing are just as important as the issue that you are organizing around. Choosing a decision-making structure for your group early on will help ease tense situations—for example, when you have twenty activists in a room with twenty different individual opinions, each of which can be argued for and reasoned through. Articulating your structure and decision-making process, and identifying an organizational mission, will go a long way toward eliminating friction during the life span of your group. Conversely, not talking or thinking about structure and process may create a situation in which unspoken issues become a source of tension and the cause of internal misunderstandings. When tension or conflict arises, as they inevitably do in human relationships, it's important to have a foundation that articulates the parameters of acceptable behavior and that can guide you toward a resolution.

STRUCTURE

As your campaign gains momentum or as your supporters multiply in number, it may be tempting to codify an organizational structure that places prominent members or early participants in positions of power or to immediately elect officers with primary decision-making capabilities. Please think about this before you proceed. You must establish a structure that best facilitates the vision and priorities of the group.

Here are some issues to consider when forming your organization:

- How are democratic decision-making processes used? Should members vote on policy? Use consensus? Will you elect or hire leaders or staff to make these decisions?
- How can new members become involved in the decision-making process?
- If officers are elected, what is the length of their term? If members assign or volunteer for specific roles or responsibilities via a consensus process, is there a mechanism for the group to assess whether the distribution of tasks has been successful?
- How are members, leaders, and volunteers held accountable by the organization?
- Should there be a mechanism to replace or recall members, volunteers, and leaders who are not fulfilling their responsibilities?

You should also think about whether your organizational structure allows your group to capitalize on participants' skills and strengths. Is there a place in your organization for people with unique skill sets or who have specific organizational strengths? Will volunteers and participants be assigned to roles at random? Is there a chance that new volunteers will be given responsibilities they are not suited for? Although it's imperative that busywork gets done and the most onerous tasks be shared and/or rotated, participants should also have the ability to donate their talents to the campaign freely. In return, your campaign will benefit from using the best that people have to give. You will also find it easier to complete tasks and garner volunteers if you are offering genuine participatory roles that are attractive to potential supporters or meaningful to dedicated members. Those dedicated members often feel a great sense of honor in being given difficult, important, or even seemingly impossible tasks. It is a great aspect of human nature that we want to give our best to our comrades, and this is a key resource for activism. Recognize it publicly when people rise to the occasion and they will astonish you with their dedication.

LEADERSHIP

There will be times when you have to just buckle down and be a leader. If people are looking for direction, don't be afraid to give it to them. Sometimes people want to be told what to do. They may want to help but not be sure of how best to do that. If they want to be involved in policy discussions, great. If they just want to hold signs and shout slogans, that is OK too. Invest yourself in your people, but don't be afraid to point them in the right direction and run toward your goal pulling them along after you.

It is very easy to become attached to historical methods of organizing or to maintain reliance on a campaign strategy that has worked in the past. Beware of becoming entrenched in routine or tradition, or of resisting organizational change. Your organization must have the courage to change directions, to adapt to new scenarios, and to relinquish roles in a situation when the current ways of doing things are no longer tenable.

This specifically applies to organizational change. Organizations are living, breathing organisms that change according to the combined temperaments of members, external pressures and adversities, shifting political winds, and the inevitable passage of time. A healthy organization will ideally cultivate an environment in which leadership roles are shared, conflict is openly discussed and resolved, and responsibilities are rotated to avoid burnout. Your goal is to lead a successful advocacy campaign for public libraries in your community. Long-term leadership requires organizational strength and the ability to withstand leadership changes and internal tensions without losing momentum.

You will want to prioritize action over organizational navel-gazing. Is your group spending more time in boring, ritualized meetings, griping over the minutiae of small things, than you are actually out in your community building a movement of library supporters? Your decision-making process (e.g., meetings, discussions) should be the means, not the end. The end is the actual active work of a campaign: organizing, advocating, and building a movement. If you are noticing that your meetings are frustrating, endless, and fruitless, consider instituting some time limits on the meeting themselves. Think about having a moderator serve at each meeting to help keep the conversation on track, avoid repetition, and guide the decision-making process toward actual goals and resolutions.

It is not absolutely necessary for your group to create an elaborate set of guidelines and rules in order to be effective. You may have a small core of organizers decide issues and strategies in a less formal manner and handle conflicts as they arise, or you may have a large group of loosely affiliated individuals who come together to raise awareness of public library issues, taking their cues from a friends-of-the-library group or the library system itself. An overemphasis on creating and defending an organizational structure can also lead to internal paralysis and can impede action and participation. Organizations and their participants may cultivate obsessions with ritual or cling to articulated roles, which can be used to block democratic processes or stifle dissent.

If, however, your organization chooses to codify a more formal structure, such as a 501(c)(3) nonprofit, a 501(c)(4) social welfare group, or a political action committee (PAC), you must adhere to legally required structures and decision-making processes. Take this into account when assessing your organizational vision and strategy.

GETTING OFFICIAL

Once you have determined your organizational goals and structure, it will be easier to decide whether you want to formalize your group through incorporation or another legal registration process. This is a big step, but it affords you a lot of legitimacy and opens up a lot of possibilities. If you want to apply for or disburse grants, raise funds, influence the political process in a formal way, hire paid staff, or build supporting programs, it may be in your best interest to form a limited liability corporation that protects leaders and participants from legal liability.

Conversely, going through these required processes may be more trouble than it's worth, sucking up immense amounts of time and preventing you from clearly assessing the appropriate role of your group in a campaign. Legal fees alone can be prohibitive, and completing the attendant paperwork can be a full-time job. It is possible to do an incredible amount of work without adopting these legal structures. In addition, your organization always has the option to shift gears and adopt a more formal structure as it grows.

501(c)3 and 501(c)4

The 501(c)(3) status is an Internal Revenue Service–designated tax exemption for nonprofit organizations. Basically, this is for organizations that want to take an active, nonpolitical role in the advocacy process, that is, by promoting literacy and public libraries in the community. Filing for tax-exempt status or incorporating requires the assistance of a lawyer and entails regular paperwork to maintain a designation. The library has a wide variety of books on incorporation and achieving tax-exempt status. If your group wants to get involved in the political arena and support (or work against) specific policies or candidates, this is not the path to take. For example, public libraries that are 501(c)(3) organizations are prevented from taking an active role in elections or legislation campaigns (and one of the reasons libraries forbid petitions at the reference desk). Your group may want to fill that void by actively lobbying for legislation that benefits libraries and supporting candidates that are library advocates. If entering the political arena and influencing voters are primary objectives, a 501(c)(3) is not for you. A 501(c)(4) might work instead. This classification includes civic leagues and social welfare groups. These groups can lobby and pursue political aims, but donations to them are not tax deductible (although the organization itself is tax exempt).

Political Action Committees

If your organization wants to support and fund-raise for (or against) candidates and legislation that affect libraries, it may want to consider forming a political action committee (PAC). There are two kinds of PACs: connected (these are connected to a specific organization or corporation and solicit donations only from members) and unconnected. Single-issue and ideological campaigns generally fall under the unconnected designation and can accept money from individuals, other PACs, and organizations.

Groups wishing to form PACs to influence federal elections must register with the Federal Election Commission and submit monthly reports of disbursements and donations. Moreover, PACs operating within state or local elections must also adhere to state guidelines. Check with your state's board of elections for more information. As with tax-exempt status, registering as a PAC requires the assistance of a lawyer and should not be taken on lightly. If your organization would like to influence the political process directly, but does not want to assume the legal responsibility of a PAC, then it should consider supporting a local PAC that donates to candidates who support libraries.

POLITICAL ACTION COMMITTEES

Federal election campaign laws—www.fec.gov/law/feca/feca.pdf
Federal Election Commission's FAQ on PACs—www.fec.gov/ans/answers_pac.shtml
New York State PAC law—www.elections.ny.gov/PAC.html

KEEPING IT SIMPLE

Does all this information about PAC and incorporation make your head hurt? Then feel free to shelve it. Return to it later—or don't. The value in bypassing these formal organizational designations is the freedom to act dynamically, to change strategies, and to operate under the radar. Your organization may decide to leave fund-raising to the library systems and friends-of-the-library groups that are set up to facilitate this and to leave overt political action to the parties and PACs that already exist in your community. You can still exert a lot of influence without the governmental formality.

Many organizations have great campaigns, rallies, and success without filing any paperwork at all. Try to get a feel for how much protection you think you might need and how much of a full-time job you can afford to make this, and then go from there.

DEFINING YOURSELF TO THE PUBLIC

Once your group has done the essential foundational work of identifying your goals and organizational structure, it is time to create a strategy for communicating your organizational identity to the public and elected officials. A coherent and consistent organizational identity is crucial to building public trust in your brand, speaking to your target audience(s), assuming your desired role in the advocacy conversation, and ultimately winning the fight for public libraries in your community.

Defining yourself to the public first requires that your group identify its target audience(s). Target audience! "What do you mean?" you might be asking. "My target audience includes elected and appointed decision makers and the voters they answer to." In this you are absolutely correct, but the reality is also a little more complex. Within every community, there are myriad small interest groups and stakeholders that most likely hold wildly divergent views on the ideal role of local government, appropriate tax policy, and essential public services. Providing free access to information and addressing the needs of youth, the poor, the unemployed, and members of other groups the library serves may be more important to some people than to others. If an advocacy campaign is to succeed, you must identify each group and formulate a strategy that addresses and speaks to its concerns. Remember, your goal is to turn opponents into allies, no matter how personally reprehensible you may find their political and ethical opinions. Every community member is a potential library supporter. Every community member retains the right to high-quality library service, whether he or she likes it or not.

It is essential that in determining your mission and organizational identity, you also identify your group's role in the advocacy conversation and stick to it. In the heat of the campaign it is alarmingly easy to find yourself caught in a political quagmire between competing interests and priorities. To keep library issues front and center and avoid getting sucked into partisanship and infighting, we recommend that you articulate (if only internally) your group's role in the activism battle. If your primary goal is to get a bond issue passed or to prevent library closures and layoffs, then speak to and organize around those issues.

Who you are is just as important as what you will eventually do. Doing the necessary work of identifying organizational identity, structure, mission, and goals will help you when you sit down to plan an event, moderate a public meeting, write a press release, talk to an elected official, or create community coalitions in support of library services. In the following three chapters, we get down to the nitty-gritty of developing an activist marketing strategy, maintaining healthy organizational relationships, building a movement of allies, and hitting the streets to promote and defend public library services in your community. You've made it to the trenches and dug in—now it's time to go over the top and engage.

2

MESSAGE AND VISIBILITY

You are what you speak. Your message will define you. It is how people outside of your group will see you, and it is ultimately how you will accomplish your goal. Most of activism is about message. We have to convince other people that what we advocate is what should be done, and if enough people accept the message, then change happens, votes are cast, and budgets get realigned. Message has always been the center of activism, and everything your organization does should be focused on getting that message out. All your marches, read-ins, rallies, photo ops, letters to the editor, and interviews should be seen only as venues for spreading the word. Petitions, postcards, and testimonials are a chance to have the community echo that message back. Hopefully that echo will eventually be loud enough to create pressure for your cause.

CREATING A MESSAGE

Your message should relate directly back to those goals and objectives you discussed when you established your group at the outset. What is it that you want to accomplish? Why are you putting in this time and effort? Is there a specific budget vote or referendum that you are targeting? The more specific you can be the better. "Yay for libraries!" is a great daily personal mantra, but it's too diffuse to attract public attention. People have been hearing that for years, since they themselves were at storytime. While they are not necessarily against you, the public knows the story already. Nobody is going to disagree with more storytime for kids, but people may discount it within the broader context of massive budget issues at all levels of government.

Crafting your message is a constantly evolving process that combines creative exploration and coldhearted calculation. Start off by focusing on your goal (e.g., school libraries in every school, a new branch, no layoffs). What do you want at the end of this campaign? What would the perfect result be? How about the worst-case scenario? What are the stakes? What happens if you fail? Write it all up, and play around with it a little. Don't focus on finding the answers immediately. Try to think like your opponents. What arguments will they have? How will they respond to what you have to say?

COMMUNICATING THE MESSAGE
TO THE FRONT LINE

Next, get your group on board with your message and procedure. As much as we emphasize empowering all members of the group, it is important that everyone knows to defer media questions to central organizers or media contacts. Those people will have press kits on hand, contacts, photo release information, and so on, and will be able to promptly coordinate interviews with organizers and stakeholders. The first thing on-the-ground supporters should do is to point the press to your media contact. Then supporters can say something positive about the library, read-in, protest, parade, or vote.

It is crucial that you divorce yourself from your message and try to look at it from the perspective of someone who has never heard of your issue and has no stake in it whatsoever. Does your message pull them in, give them the story, persuade them to your side, and indicate the stakes of potential loss if these efforts should fail? You might be fighting for your life's work, the ideal of the library, the library you grew up in, a sense of justice, or your family's livelihood, but the simple fact is that the man or woman on the street may not care about any of that. He or she will probably harbor your cause no ill will, but indifference will be of no help to you either. You need to have a message that will stop people in their tracks, win them over to your side, and have them talking about it at their dinner table that night.

What are some tricks? Think about the losses, and dwell on them. Who really wants to get behind something that will kill children's literacy? Who actually wants to stop programming for elderly shut-ins? Get those awful realities that the library sheds some hope on and grind them in people's faces. Play on higher issues of justice, free speech, and education, but tie them closely to people's own home turf. *Local* history is at stake; *this* community's cultural storehouse is under attack. Opposite to the not-in-my-backyard principle, you have to make your cause very in my backyard. Put the issue where people live, and make them see it as a fight they have a stake in. People like value for their money, so focus on how much the library can save them. If a new property tax for the library will raise taxes by an average of $30 annually, point out that that is the cost of a book, and offer to loan them a thousand books this year for free to make it up. People like to be proud of themselves, so let them know the innovative things you are doing in the community, and let them vicariously take credit for it. "Without your public support, of course, none of this would be possible" is a great, almost-pat line. It is also true, so why not let people know it? Make people feel good about the library, and they will want to do good by the library. Make them feel that supporting your cause is the right thing to do, and they will feel better about themselves every time they advocate on your behalf.

It is important that you have some things prepared for different circumstances and schedules. You may have all the time in the world to lay out the merits of broad-based library services to the community, or you might have ten seconds to attract someone's attention and get that person to consider your side. Have a short, snappy summary when you approach people, and don't be afraid to use lines such as the following:

- "Do you use the library?" (asked of someone exiting the library with an armload of books and media)
- "Do you think that culture and the arts have a place in [name your town, city, county]?"
- "Do you support early childhood education?"

Such questions may seem overused or even manipulative, but they will get people to stop for a conversation.

CONNECTING WITH THE PUBLIC ONLINE

Developing a resonating message is only part of the equation. You are charged with the task of communicating it to current and potential supporters. Although face-to-face outreach will always be a priority, you must conduct outreach digitally as well. Social-networking sites are some of the best tools library advocates have for effective activism. These tools provide easy ways to find and communicate with your supporters and to spread the word about what your library needs. With so many people using the Internet in every community, it really is the most effective and efficient way to spread the word. Library supporters are everywhere—all you need to do is find them, and they'll be happy to help.

Once you've decided that you are going to use social networking tools to support your activism, you need to decide which platforms you want to use. You'll want to take into account your budget and how much time you have to commit to the online portion of your campaign. Most of the tools we consider here are free, but you could go whole hog and get a web designer. See what skills your supporters have, and you might be able to find someone who can donate his or her time.

Social media is more than a passing fad. It is a valuable set of communication tools. These social networks create large, interconnected webs of individuals linked by common interests and friendship and familial groupings. Social-networking tools allow you to tap into these webs and provide instantaneous and widespread communication. That communication can be used for organizing, energizing, and informing people to come out for real action. The real power of social media comes from the quick, easy, word-of-mouth marketing that it encourages. That's what you're tapping into when you use social networking for communications.

Social media use is growing by leaps and bounds. There are staggering numbers of people out there using these tools. In 2009, 55.6 million adults visited a social-networking site at least once a month in the United States.[1] That's one-third of the adult population. Facebook reports 500 million users worldwide in 2011,[2] and by 2010 Twitter was reporting usage statistics of 50 million tweets per day.[3] If you're concerned about reaching older portions of the population, don't be. The Pew Research Center reports that the fastest-growing group of social network users is those older than age sixty-five, followed closely by those between the ages of fifty and sixty-four.[4]

> ### A SUCCESSFUL CAMPAIGN
>
> In Buffalo, New York, the librarians started a Facebook profile for Save the BECPL (the Buffalo and Erie County Public Library) and reached out to more than a thousand supporters. They organized rallies and call-ins, and they sent a slew of letters to the editor of the local paper. By the time they were done, backing the proposed cuts was political suicide. The campaign successfully clawed back $3 million out of a $4 million proposed budget cut, despite a promised veto by local politicians.

Give this stuff some thought at the outset and as you go forward. Web 2.0 is not advocacy's magic bullet. It is important to consider things like which social-networking tools your community uses most. Look around, and start asking friends and family how they spend their time online. That should give you a good idea of where to start. If most of your local community uses MySpace, for example, a Facebook page won't be very useful, and vice versa.

Social-networking tools are fantastic, but they should be used purposefully. Creating a Facebook page and posting comments isn't enough to get you what you want. Effective activism always includes something real and physical. Use your social-networking following to coordinate real-life activism. Build your online community with the intention that your new friends will come out for rallies, write letters, and make phone calls. Your goal is *not* to have one thousand likes for your campaign's Facebook page. Your goal is to get one thousand people contacting their representatives, attending events, signing petitions, and physically demonstrating their commitment and support of public libraries. Facebook and Twitter are tools to facilitate that goal. They are the means to achieve the end; they are not the end itself. If the sole function of your group is the maintenance of a Facebook page, you are doing it wrong.

WORKING WITH THE PRESS

A carefully cultivated relationship with the media is essential to a successful campaign. You cannot afford to create an event, start your campaign, rally your troops, and then cross your fingers and hope that a newspaper, radio show, or blog hears about your group and contacts you for your perspective. If that is your media strategy, then you're going to have very limited exposure and the campaign will ultimately be unsuccessful. To maximize your reach, you must prioritize your relationship with the media and attend to it with the same care that you would afford your relationship with politicians and community leaders.

The first step in cultivating media relationships is to figure out whom to talk to. Develop a list (see "Media Contact Tracker" in the appendixes at the back of the book) of media contacts for an array of print, web, radio, and television resources. This way you can easily access the contact information the moment you have a press release or media blurb to disseminate. Using a shared spreadsheet for your organization (as in Google Docs) will allow members to share responsibilities and track e-mails without duplicating effort.

In the beginning, you may likely be dependent on the basic info@yournewspaper type of addresses found on websites. Over time, and as your leads are picked up by media outlets, you will have the opportunity to develop a rapport with specific reporters, columnists, and editors. Always keep track of their names and job descriptions, and use the spreadsheet to track your previous interactions with them. Building a mutually respectful and beneficial relationship with a media contact will pay off for your organization in the end and protect you when you are fighting heated and pitched battles for the hearts and minds of your community.

Building that mutually beneficial relationship with a media contact is not just about trying to wrangle positive press for your organization and library campaign. It is about giving the media contact the inside scoop on the issue, and giving that contact the time, access, and insight that he or she needs to write a good story. There may be media outlets in your community that you identify as opposed to library funding. This is your chance to approach editors, writers, or reporters and let them know why libraries are important to them and to their audience. There is a saying that all press is good press, but that is debatable. Sometimes reporters may have an ax to grind or a story already written in their head before they even begin their interviews. If a reporter seems to have an agenda or is fishing for quotes, then tread carefully. At the same time, there is really no way to tell, so answer everyone in good faith and if a reporter misquotes you, then he or she is the bad guy, not you. Work hard at making the stories that are about the library and your movement are good stories. Of course, you want them to speak well of you and your cause, but also try to make the story interesting.

You have the responsibility of reaching out to the community through the press in its many forms and convincing reporters of public libraries' essential value in a language that is understandable to them and accessible to the writer. If the story resonates, you will become a trusted source for the media outlet and the recipient of early-morning phone calls and e-mails asking for response quotes. Take a second to think about what they are asking you before you give them a quote. See what you can find out about the story they are writing, and consider whether it is something that you really want to weigh in on. If they are doing a piece about literacy rates in your town and what can be done to improve them, great. If they are doing a hatchet job on the mayor or writing an article about how community reading rooms can take the place of public libraries, then consider fobbing them off with a simple, "You know, I have never really thought of it, and that is not something that our organization really gets involved in." Take the time to ask a few questions yourself, and you can potentially save yourself a lot of head-aches in the end. In any case, always be quick to respond to the press, and be gracious even when you are saying nothing. When the time comes to promote your event or cause, the person on the other end of the line will remember how you responded to the previous call.

PRESS RELATIONS 101

Developing a press relationship gives you the opportunity to frame the issue. By this time, you should already know the mission, purpose, and strategy of your organization, and have a thorough understanding of the library issues involved. If you don't have answers to at least some of these, then consider flipping back to the beginning of this book and taking the time to put everything on paper. What you are doing is writing your elevator speech: the speech that is short enough to say in the time it takes an elevator to go between floors. You should be able to convey your core message concisely. Distill your message down to three or four main points that you can return to in interviews.

Take the time to tailor your message to its intended recipients and identify the appropriate vehicles for particular stories. Always take into account speed of publishing! For instance, if you need to get the word out about a particularly weighty development that requires immediate action, then reach out to bloggers, daily newspapers, and radio or television. Weekly or monthly print outlets may be more interested in giving a broad overview of the history of library funding in your community than an issue necessitating quick response. They might do an in-depth story, but you will need to be in touch earlier, even months ahead of your crisis.

If you have had positive interactions with particular reporters or writers, then by all means notify them of momentous developments. They will remember and come to you when it is time to write about library issues. Give them a shot at a really good story, and they will remember you when you ask them for help later on.

WRITING YOUR PRESS RELEASE

Take the time to write an engaging and accurate press release. More often than not, a journalist will use the statistics and facts that you cite without verifying them. You have a vested interest in providing accurate data that support your case for continued or increased funding. In addition, you should include other crucial components that convey information about your organization and campaign. Be sure to get the who, what, when, where, and how in there. Your press release should contain the following:

- Press contact information: The person listed as the contact should be comfortable with public speaking and be prepared to answer questions and conduct interviews related to the press release, often with very little notice. If you put your own contact info on the press release, you will want to use a cell phone number and an e-mail address that you check frequently. The news cycle is getting ever shorter, and you will be doing journalists a huge favor if you can respond to their questions quickly or help them make a deadline by the end of the day.
- Website: You should have this up already, even if it's only a skeleton site holder.
- The background of the issue: historical library funding trends, budget issues—you need to provide context.

- Your mission: Who is your group? Why do they care?
- Your goal: Full funding, obviously, but also provide specifics. What are you fighting?
- Facts and statistics: Numbers are your friend. Cite dollar amounts and library use statistics to back up your arguments.
- What you want people to do: Who is the target of this public pressure? Who makes the decisions? What can people do to help you or get involved?
- The immediate event at hand: Were layoff notices handed out? Are you hosting a rally in protest of the budget cuts? Are you responding to a speech?

Your numbers must, must, must be accurate. If you are citing another person's research, be prepared to provide the source if questioned. Do not exaggerate beyond a reasonable rounding up or down of numbers. You don't have to create doomsday scenarios; they may well already be there. Describe the consequences of the proposed legislation, budget cuts, or failure to repair or update library facilities. Describe what happened in the past when library budgets were cut, or describe a time when your city or town did not have the library facilities it does now. If your town has minimal services, contrast it with nearby municipalities with similar economic situations but better library resources. It would also help if those towns are high school football rivals.

In addition to your basic press release, you may want to write a special release for a specific audience—parents, seniors, local artists, entrepreneurs, business leaders. Tailor your message accordingly. This is a good opportunity for you to target potential allies and inform them about how library cuts will specifically affect them. You may also want to write a blog press release to share with other bloggers. This may be shorter and newsier, and contain links to statistics and quotes, digital images, and artwork. It can serve as a ready-made blog post that your source can modify as needed.

Continue to reach out to newspapers. Take a moment to ask a reporter about the print schedule. If a weekly newspaper goes to print on Friday and it is Wednesday night, then make sure your contact has the information he or she needs as soon as possible, even if it means you don't get around to e-mailing the bloggers until tomorrow. Taking everyone's schedule into account and understanding the timing of the news cycle will ultimately benefit your organization's exposure.

INTERVIEWS

Interviews with the media give you the opportunity to deliver a more targeted version of your elevator speech. Practice mock interviews with your group so that you are all prepared to give short statements and state the main points of your argument. You must be able to stay on message no matter what the interviewer asks. This is your opportunity to communicate your passion and the importance of public libraries directly to the community. Be prepared to be your library's mouthpiece and leave your shyness at the door.

TELEVISION

Television is an amazing way to get your word out. Don't be nervous about it, but do prepare for it. First off, the obvious—please check your reflection in a mirror before you go on camera. As a community organizer, you are not expected to look super polished, but it is crucial that you have the basics covered: nothing in your teeth, no food on your shirt. Breathe. Smile. Make your point quickly, preferably in ten seconds or less. Keep coming back to your message, and deliver it convincingly but in tiny, tiny bits. Remember that news segments are short and heavily edited, so try to maximize your small amount of screen time. Be aware beforehand that the camera is likely to be about one or two feet from your face. Don't stare at it. Look at the person you are talking to. If you have the option, you may as well try to get the camera pointed at your good side (everyone has one).

RADIO

A radio interview is a luxury, especially if the setup allows call-ins, where you phone in to the radio program from the comfort of your home or office, and you can lay out cheater blurbs for reference. Remember to ask about your listening audience and the length of the segment beforehand. If the show is not live, your comments will likely be edited down, so try to include snappy phrases and vivid imagery to make an impression. If a member of your group is particularly gregarious or has a melodious voice, utilize him or her. Don't let a group member who speaks in a monotone or has a hard time making the case take on this job.

PRINT

As with other media outlets, be aware of whom you are speaking with and what the particular slant of the publication is, and address these perspectives in your responses. Remember that for many people, print media is still the most authoritative and valid source for news and facts. In some cities and towns, the local newspaper heavily covers local political issues, with specific reporters assigned to beats. You might be surprised how much the reporter knows about library issues and city funding, so bone up on the background and specifics before the interview or event so that you can be the authority on the subject.

BLOGS

How many local news blogs have popped up in your area in the past few years? If you take the time to look, you may be surprised. With so many local papers going under, ordinary citizens are filling the void. You can find local blogs on general news and announcements, or alternately, blogs that are dedicated to a limited subject matter. Many of these local news blogs have extensive readerships, and where there is also a local paper, the reporters sometimes get their scoops from blogs. Treat bloggers the same way you would a newspaper reporter. Make sure you have a grasp on the slant their stories take before you speak to them, and read through some of their archived posts. Some bloggers will be interested in doing extensive writing for your cause; some may just report event announcements from your website. Both of these approaches are fine, and helpful.

Your Blog

You should be creating your own press: publishing unfiltered missives and position posts on your organization's website or blog that represent your message and take on the issues. Obviously, you should be chasing down those press leads and cultivating relationships with reporters and bloggers, but you don't have to sit around and wait for someone to write about what you are doing. You can create the story yourself.

The best content sources are your supporters. Take the time to solicit their perspectives and get them to tell your story for you. That may sound like too much work but it doesn't have to be. This is another excellent opportunity for you to reach out to allies and pull them into the advocacy fold. Ask a supporter to write a quick blurb on how they use the library, or their favorite library memories, or their response to a recent event relating to library funding. Ask some local authors for their favorite books as children. Ask an illustrator to draw a graphic for a heading. Ask a community leader to guest blog with an op-ed. There are many ways to reduce the direct writing load on your organization, but they all begin with asking friends for help.

Creating buzz or getting out quick responses to recent campaign developments doesn't necessarily require an entire blog post. This is what Facebook and Twitter are for—steadily kicking out short, bite-sized nuggets that can be repeated and shared. These can spur on-the-ground action, complement your overall media strategy, and keep your issue prominent in people's eyes. Make sure to balance your reliance on social media within your overall strategy. You must reach large segments of the community that may not be in your social network or use Web 2.0 tools as a primary source of local news information.

MARKETING TOOLS

Marketing really is just about selling a feeling. If people hear the word *library* and feel all warm and fuzzy, then you're good! Your message and imagery should always correspond to your unique needs and circumstances. Think about tone in design the same way you would think about tone in writing, and match it up with your message. If your general tone is very doom and gloom, think about using dark tones and fonts with serifs, like Times New Roman and Courier. Happy messages can come with bright cheerful colors and sans-serif fonts like Arial. Don't underestimate the effects of a good font choice.

It's important to connect all of your different marketing tools with the same theme. The theme includes not only your message but also your logo, tag lines, colors, and overall vibe. How you choose to represent your organization should be consistent throughout your entire campaign. Use your logo and tag line on everything from your flyers to your website and Facebook page.

Images, graphics, and colors are an easy way to make your group identifiable. They can draw people to look at your materials and give your issue more thought, and they can help you properly convey information. If viewers have to search for the information they want, your material does not work. Times and dates of events should be prominent and easily located. Don't try to cram too much into the space, and be sure everything is clearly legible and spelled correctly. Once the basics are in place, your design can really shine.

Take the time to really think about the type of marketing materials that appeal to you. What made you stop and look further? What prompted you to take the time to look up an advertised URL? Use these ideas as inspiration for your own work. Apple is an excellent example of good, simple graphics. The viewer sees everything in the first few seconds of looking at an advertisement of an Apple product. That's what you want, for the viewer to get your point immediately.

Flags, Buttons, and More

It's easy to describe physical marketing tools—they are the first thing that comes to mind when you imagine a rally. Flyers, signs, buttons, and T-shirts are all physical ways to get your message out. Uniting them all with your common image or color scheme really reinforces your message, and it makes the materials identifiable as belonging to your group. This is a great place to have fun as an activist. Use this as an opportunity to juice up your creative powers. Make lots of different banners and signs—uniform, mass-produced ones, no matter how well designed, can look prepackaged side by side at a rally. Have fun with different slogans and images. At the same time, do a quick check of your supporters to be sure that nobody in your crowd is holding a sign that you would not want on the front page of the local paper the next day. "Save Storytime" with a teddy bear is good, "The Mayor Is a Monster" with a Photoshopped image of her with vampire fangs is not so good.

Break out the button maker you use for summer reading, and fire up your sewing machines to hem banners. Stencils and spray paint work great for banners, flags, and really guerrilla T-shirts. You can get better shirts made up at a local screen-printing shop or even make them yourself if you or someone in your organization has that skill. Dress your people up, give them signs to wave and banners to walk behind—this creates an image, a brand, for you. These trappings are part of what make a political movement fun and get you in the papers. A bunch of people standing together is a crowd. Put signs in their hands and you have a rally. Give them matching T-shirts and it is a movement.

VIRTUAL TOOLS

There are three major types of web tools that will be most useful to activists, traditional websites or blogs, microblogging clients like Facebook or Twitter, and e-mail. It is important to use them all to reach as many people as possible. Make sure to keep your logo, colors, and general tone consistent between virtual and physical materials.

A website or blog gives your organization a home on the Internet, providing a stable location where people can find you and learn what your group is all about. Having an independent website allows you to control the look and content, and you can use it as a base for information distributed elsewhere. If your site is kept up to date, it can be a great place to refer people to for exact statistics and in-depth information. Instead of writing similar stories on all of your web accounts, you can simply link to your blog or website. The blog format is particularly useful for library advocates, because it allows you to update supporters on a continuing basis. Most web-based blogging software is free to use. Be forewarned, if you choose a free service, you'll notice that they are usually supported by small ads, which may or may not be in line with your cause. You can usually get perks like a hosted domain name or ad-free sites for a small fee. Check your blogging platform's help pages to find out how.

Microblogging clients like Facebook and Twitter provide an easy platform for reaching out to supporters in a way that simply can't be done with a regular website or blog. You'll be amazed at how much you can say in 140 characters. Activism is built on relationships, and these tools allow you to build on and use those relationships to build support for your issue. One of the best aspects of microblogging sites is the ability of users to share things they find interesting, like photos links or events.

Don't forget e-mail. E-mail is still the best way to communicate directly with individuals, and it can't be ignored. It's a good idea to create a dedicated e-mail for your organization so the public and press can reach you easily. It can be free to start an account on a service like Yahoo! or Gmail, and it's well worth doing.

Besides individual communication, you can also use e-mail for mass mailings. It can be a great way to remind people of events right before they happen. There are a few ways to go about this. You can use a regular e-mail client, but you may have restrictions on the amount of recipients per e-mail, or you can use an e-mail marketing service. These allow you to comply with federal laws regarding e-mail spam and make it easy to create and send attractive, professional-looking e-mails. These services can come with a fee, which is generally reasonable but may be out of reach if you don't have a budget.

VIDEO

Videos can be an excellent outreach tool. They are really easy to post and share on the Internet. If you use a hosting site like YouTube, you can insert the embedding code in your blog or website and share the video on social-networking sites as well. There are a lot of things you can do with video. You can record events or create Internet public-service announcements. Making a funny video can help raise awareness for your campaign. Videos are cheap and easy to produce, especially with open-source video-editing software. For this sort of video editing you only need basic capabilities like cutting and adding credits. You may be lucky enough to have supporters with video-editing skills. Utilize them! In fact, you can use people with all sorts of skills to help you make a video. Why not make it a community project? Take the skills of your supporters—music, writing, video editing, the ability to get out of a straitjacket—and put them to use.

If you end up editing the video yourself, here are a few basics to get you started:

- Keep it simple. Don't let fancy transitions and animations detract from your message.
- Pay attention to the sound balance. If the music overwhelms your dialogue, viewers will miss your point.
- Use credits. You don't just have to use them to say who made the film; you can also use them to spell out what the video is about, to thank politicians who have supported you, and to make announcements.
- Make sure to cite any music or images you have used in the ending credits.

Streaming video of your events can be a fun and easy way to engage your supporters. Not everyone will be able to make it to every event. Posting live video of a rally or other event means that people who are at work or out of the area can watch it in real time and still feel engaged. Clearly, it can't be the same as having those people actually be present, but enabling remote participation can help build excitement and goodwill. Live streaming an event also provides a record that you can use to produce other videos or to show elected officials that two hundred people really did show up.

If you can use a smartphone and Facebook, then you can produce streaming video. There are several services that provide free streaming video and phone apps. If you take the time to set it up before hand, you can embed a video player into your website and let people know that you will be recording the event. You can also use a laptop and web cam if you have an event that can be recorded from a stationary camera.

Posting and sharing online videos are great ways to get your cause noticed, so go crazy! Charlotte-Mecklenberg, North Carolina, did some amazing videos of zombie protests, and the New York Public Library's "Ghostbusters" video got major mainstream press coverage. Even if they don't go viral, creating videos can be a good way to break up your content and keep supporters interested. They are easy to share, and thanks to new technologies, they are very cheap and simple to make. With a basic mini-camera and free software, you can create a great little PSA video.

> Charlotte-Mecklenberg's Zombies for Libraries website: http://zombiesforlibraries.com
> New York Public Library's "Ghostbusters" video: www.nypl.org/audiovideo/who -you-gonna-call

Think of your favorite commercials and what makes them effective. They are usually simple, straightforward, and a little bit funny, right? So aim for that. You want your message to be obvious, but you definitely need some sort of hook. The video could be made by library staff or patrons, or maybe teens. Reach out to the local community and get them involved.

Live streaming video is a great option for protests. Webcasting events like this is more involved, but you can recruit a tech person who can take care of this for you.

Frankly, this is getting so easy that you may not even need that. Many webcasting services are also free. We streamed our 24-Hour Read-In event live on our blog and got more than six hundred page views in that twenty-four-hour period. There were viewers not only from all over the city but from different parts of the country as well. It's a great way to involve supporters who can't be present in real life.

GRAPHICS

No event or campaign is complete without graphics. Visuals are very important. They help the public remember who you are and can grab their attention. You want people who are walking by your flyers or rally to stop and look, and strong graphics can help with that. Remember, the library probably isn't the only organization facing cuts, so no effort you make to grab people's eyes is wasted. Go for bold designs and colors, if color is possible. Try to avoid clip art, since the image isn't there to fill a space but to do a job. Make sure your graphics directly relate to libraries. If a graphic has to be explained, then it isn't making your point for you.

Building Relationships with Content Creators

Don't forget the artists in your community. They are often avid library users and can really help to make your campaign stand out. Visual artists can make arresting images that will help people remember you. Writers can literally spread the word and make compelling cases on your behalf. Local filmmakers may want to get involved, and this is an incredibly compelling medium. At the same time, you must be aware of your library's privacy and photography policies when dealing with filmmakers, documentary makers, or still photographers and respect those policies at all times. Reach out to local galleries or theaters, but be sensitive to the fact that they may be looking at their own funding worries. Who knows, maybe you can help one another.

Artists and creative types can also add a great deal of cachet to your events. Having musicians at a protest is an amazing way to fill time, draw a crowd, and give your event impact. Dramatic types may provide you with street theater that will move your protest to the front page. You will find library allies everywhere. Be open to the wide variety of skill sets that they can contribute to your movement and embrace them when they crop up.

SOCIAL MEDIA TIED TO ACTION

Just like posting your bra color won't cure breast cancer, posting "I Love Libraries" over and over on your Facebook feed won't get your funding restored, and it will probably cost you some Facebook friends. Doing outreach on the Internet isn't enough. You need to get people out in the streets, talking to public officials, and testifying at hearings.

Ask around, think about what makes you stop and read an article or Facebook status. Use your social-networking presence to put out real, timely useful information. Link to articles related to what you are fighting for. Post your events and promote your blog posts. The people who are following you on these sites are doing so because they want this information from you. Try to give it to them in a clear concise way, so that they keep coming back. Social media is just that, social. Start and participate in conversations, build relationships, dispel rumors, and solicit ideas. You never know who will come up with the next amazing rally idea.

Don't forget to give people something solid to do. This is what moves them from Facebook followers to activists. A post that says, "Save the Library!" will get lots of approval but doesn't really do much. Instead, say, "Save the library by coming to *this* rally, or by writing to *that* person, or by filling out *these* postcards." Once your followers have a task, they can be engaged rather than passive. They can shift from followers to supporters and activists.

Most important, don't be annoying. You know what we mean. Everyone has the one obnoxious friend who posts chain Facebook status updates all the time or just reposts everything that is ever written on one topic. You know the one, the friend who would be heartbroken if she ever caught on that you had given up and blocked her posts? Don't be her. People will ignore you. Be positive and proactive instead. Save the sturm und drang for later: we're saving libraries (happy places), not disabling land mines.

Human beings will always be the most effective marketing tool in your arsenal, but you still have to use additional tools to maximize your effectiveness. Building an activist strategy is about deciding how to best allocate your time and resources to tools and policies that convey your message. Over the past few pages, we discussed the nuts and bolts of outreach: fleshing out your message, communicating with supporters, representing your organization to the media and the public, and marketing your cause. In the next chapter, we discuss building the interpersonal and organizational relationships that form the bedrock of your movement.

NOTES

1. Adam Ostrow, "Number of Social Networking Users Has Doubled Since 2007," Mashable, January 29, 2009, http://mashable.com/2009/07/28/social-networking-users-us.

2. Aden Hepburn, "Facebook Statistic, Stats & Facts for 2011," *digitalbuzz* (blog), January 18, 2011, www.digitalbuzzblog.com/facebook-statistics-stats-facts-2011/.

3. "Twitter Facts & Figures (History & Statistics)," compiled by websitemonitoring.com, April 2010, www.website-monitoring-com/blog/2010/05/04/twitter-facts-and-figures-history-statistics/.

4. Janice Lloyd, "More Older Folks Jumping Online; Technology Helps Them Stay in Touch," *USA Today*, December 15, 2010.

3

NAVIGATING RELATIONSHIPS

Your allies are everywhere. One big thing you have in your favor is that libraries have a pretty good brand. People generally support the mission of lending materials, providing computer access, providing unbiased answers to complex questions, and running cultural and educational programs free of charge to every member of the general public. They get it. Reach people with your message, and they can move mountains for you.

Often your backers are ready at hand. Almost every library has its core of supporters, friends, boosters, and users who take up in support of the library when the time comes. Each of these individuals or groups may have its own vision of the library and of library activism efforts. How, then, do you get these people on board and working together? How can you get them to add their voice to your campaign and make your group's voice louder?

WORKING WITH LIBRARY ADMINISTRATION

It is important that your group's efforts coincide with the activities that your library and administration are pursuing. These kinds of fights are hard enough without inviting trouble. If you don't buck your boss or grind an ax with your director, your independent advocacy can work really well for everyone. If you are out there trying to support the library, people may not pat you on the back, but odds are they won't stand in your way. Hopefully your library is also doing something, so look for ways to assist with and augment the efforts. You want to work hand in hand as much as you can. Let the library know you are helping and united in doing work that benefits everybody.

An ideal situation is to have an independent library activist group that works in concert with an official library line. Perhaps your group can carry part of the load by arranging independent events and campaigns. Independent campaigns can be more outspoken and go farther out on a limb. They can make bolder political statements than a library might be able to do. Let your library's administration know what you are doing and what you are saying. It's never good to surprise your library or put it in an embarrassing position. Even if your relationship with the library is strained, there is no need to have the library director find out about a protest by reading about it in the

CONSTANT ADVOCACY

Library advocacy is traditionally cyclical. There is a flurry of activity around budget votes or bond issues, followed by long periods of silence in wait for the next crisis. These crises end up dominating the activist narrative, and as a result, the only time we call on the public is when we are wailing and gnashing our teeth. A constant advocacy model is a departure from the disaster response model of advocacy. Instead of reacting in a panic, advocate for the library year-round. Many of the people who are involved in this kind of activism and advocacy are library workers. These are the people who know the message; who are engaged in the practical work of libraries; and whose livelihoods will be affected by cuts in budgets, hours, and services. If you are one of these people, it is very important that the advocacy you do for libraries does not affect your professionalism as a librarian. Keep your relationships at work positive, and keep up good service at the desk. It is hard to make the case that we are essential if our work is shoddy.

Make sure that the great services your library provides are in the news even when there is not an ax hanging over them. Keep the public aware of the library's value to the community even when nobody is talking about tax dollars.

The best way to accomplish this is by being a really great library and providing people with stellar service. When libraries are short staffed and people are facing a lot of job insecurity, morale can drop and burnout can run rampant. It may be hard for people to focus on their work if they are not sure they are going to have a job. Unfortunately, that is exactly the time when superior service is critical to keeping public opinion on your side. If you make your library the crown jewel of your community and a source of local pride, it will be much harder for people who want to be reelected to cut your budget when the topic comes up for discussion.

Obviously, this is a big goal, one that goes far beyond simple activism. It is something to reach for. This is not to say you shouldn't whip people into a frenzy when big votes are coming. You absolutely must get them fired up. Constant advocacy, though, keeps the library always in the public eye, even when there's no crisis, and reinforces the idea that you are constantly striving to give the public a library it can take pride in.

---

newspaper. Keep your lines of communication open, and you will be amazed at what happens. Our organization has partnered with all three of the big library systems in New York City, and they have given us space, electricity, tents, security, water, food, and all kinds of other help. Most of all, by providing this support, the libraries gave our protests legitimacy and weight. There is not much point in protesting in support of a library system that refuses to admit you exist. Try to work hand in hand with library leadership wherever and whenever possible.

Having said that, don't let the library administration take over your campaign. Keep them apprised and engaged, but remember that you make your message. Your independent efforts can offer them a nice level of deniability while allowing them to benefit from a great deal of extra creativity and energy. It's a win-win situation if everyone is on board.

THE LIBRARY BOARDS OF TRUSTEES

Working with library boards of trustees can be tricky. Often, the administration would prefer you keep away from trustees altogether, especially if the board is very influential. Take your cue from your administration. At the same time, board members may smile on your efforts and want to help you. In some places they are very involved in advocating for the library and funding. They volunteer their time and are active library boosters just like you. They can often be found at rallies, and they can be incredibly generous in their support. Always treat them with respect, and be very grateful of the time, effort, and attention they donate on your behalf. (Bad-mouthing *anybody* who advocates for the library is not classy.) Give them a chance to participate in your campaign, and thank them profusely for anything they do or offer. Make your events fun for them, and they will remember your cause fondly.

ELECTED OFFICIALS

When it comes to libraries, your local politicians can often be found proclaiming support loud and clear. Libraries are warm and fuzzy places where smiling children learn to read, the unemployed look for work, and the elderly find reading material and social interaction. Who could be against that? Elected officials want to fund libraries and be known as library supporters. It's our job to make it easy for them.

Good elected officials respond to the concerns of their constituents. The most straightforward way to get the support of politicians is to encourage their constituents to write or call them with stories and statements in support of the library. If you've done your job crafting your message and making it clear and compelling, this part should be easy.

Deciding which elected officials to approach for support can be daunting. There are a lot of offices, and finding out who is responsible for what can be confusing. First, look at how the local government works and how funding is allocated. Are there committees within the legislative body? Is there a budget director? Find out who the chair of the library committee is, and target that person. If there isn't a library committee, look for an elected official who has spoken out in support of libraries in the past. Is there someone who has shown support for education? Libraries are the ultimate education machine; they serve everyone, so show how an interest in education aligns with support for libraries.

Gaining access to an elected official can be very hard. Officials usually have staff working very hard to keep the nuts away and keep a constant kaleidoscope of constituents and interests flowing in and out of the office. What this means is that you may have to convince a few layers of staff that you are serious about what you are doing before you can start talking to the official. This is where a good relationship with your library administration and board can be helpful. An introduction from either will make it easier to work with the office. You may have to deal with one or more staff members. The employee who is likely to be the most help is the chief of staff, who runs the office (or more than one office). Elected officials often don't manage their own schedules. Find out who keeps track of activities, and it's that person who can move things around so officials can get to your events. The press secretary takes care of press communications. The press secretary sets up interviews and goes to events with the official to make sure he or she talks to the right people. Don't be afraid to just start calling. No matter what you say to the staffer on the other end of the line, someone said something crazier to him or her about five minutes before you called. It's the staff's job to listen to constituents, and that's what you are.

It is important to have realistic expectations about what politicians can do for you. In general, an elected official is in a position to vote in the library's favor, come to events, voice support, and speak to the press on your behalf and pressure colleagues to do the same. Before approaching elected officials, have a clear plan; know what you want from them. They are probably very busy and may only have a few minutes for you. It's time to dust off your elevator speech and modify it. Are you pushing for a yes vote on a funding referendum? Trying to persuade an official to vote no on a decrease? Looking for an official able to convince colleagues to vote for your cause? No matter what you are asking for, most elected officials will appreciate a concise, clear presentation of your issue and what you want from them.

Every few years, as leaders come and go, you may have to start building new relationships. Don't stress about it—just introduce yourself and move ahead. As long as your group wasn't a major part of the opposing candidate's campaign, there shouldn't be a problem. Remember, libraries are awesome; who doesn't want to support us?

STAFF AND PROFESSIONAL GROUPS

One group of people has a vested interest in getting on board with your movement: library workers. Whether they are public library staff, employees of local schools, special or corporate librarians, MLS students, archivists, museum workers, or historical society staffers, they're your people. These are your natural allies and your troops. They understand why libraries are important. They understand exactly what libraries do. They are deeply aware of just how much is at stake when library budgets are cut. Utilize these people.

Take a moment to identify the various segments that constitute your professional audiences and the organizations that represent them. These will include public library unions, professional organizations, educators' unions that include school librarians, university programs in library science, archivist roundtables, and more. Each group will have its own culture, decision-making structure, access points, and communications apparatus. Each will have to be approached separately and with care. Most will unhesitatingly offer support, but their idea of support will be based on the function and structure of their own group. Approaching them strategically will ensure that you maintain realistic expectations and minimize misunderstandings along the way.

Assess the professional organizations in your area. Are there regional library associations? State library associations? Local professional groups operating on an ad-hoc basis? Make a list. Then, one by one, familiarize yourself with the organization's website, paying special attention to the organization's structure and activities. This information should influence how you approach the organization.

Determine your access point by finding the contact information for the individual you'd like to speak with. Is there a general contact e-mail address, or are there multiple staff e-mail addresses? You may want to attend a meeting and introduce yourself in person. Don't forget to prepare before you reach out; to avoid embarrassment, have answers to questions ready when you meet people for the first time.

Identify how the group can assist, how members can get involved, and what exactly you are asking them to do. This may include asking for general volunteers, foot soldiers for canvassing, or a receptive audience for a presentation. Whatever it is, be explicit about what you need and connect it to the mission of the organization. Most important, offer your alliance in return. If you ask for signatures on your petition, be ready to sign theirs.

If library employees are part of a labor union, the union should be an integral part of your advocacy strategy, as an ally and as a partner. It may already be preparing a campaign against library budget cuts. If so, familiarize yourself with it and join forces with the union. Make contact immediately. You need the staff union on board just as badly as you need the library administration. Make it clear that you understand that advocating for libraries means advocating for library workers. Saving jobs is always a good motivator. Discuss ways for library staff to get involved. If they can't advocate at work, help create ways for staff to become active off the clock.

Keep in mind that working with a union is different from working with a professional organization. Unions have their own history, culture, and complex relationships with library administration and local municipalities. They are democratic organizations that reflect the input and participation of members. Attempting to approach union leadership as if they were unilateral decision makers can backfire on your group and lead to stymied expectations on both ends. Reach out to the union's membership as a whole, and the entire movement will be the richer for it.

Look to the schools! Everyone loves a school librarian. Chances are you have school librarians in your community who are well known and respected, and deeply understand how important public libraries are to the children of your community. Take the time to go speak with them and figure out how you can collaborate on advocacy. They are the public figures who can loudly speak out for libraries, write letters to the editor, make speeches at rallies, and stand up at town meetings.

Don't ignore your other potential allies—future library workers. If your city or county has a library school, get on over there and talk to the students. Make it clear that keeping libraries open is crucial to their professional future. Let them use their time, energy, and enthusiasm to think up creative ways to get the word out about library budget cuts. If you are in a college town, there might be student groups interested in helping you. Stop by the schools of social work and education and see who you can get on board (don't forget to check in at the university libraries, of course). Give them the resources— petitions, postcards, event information—and let them run with them.

Last but not least, don't forget staff at local museums, archives, and historical associations. These institutions may be governed by the same municipal agency that governs your library and be threatened by the same budget cuts. Their leadership might even include leaders from your local public library. Don't view these institutions as funding competition; think of them as allies. Drop in, strike up a conversation with staff members about common interests, and take it from there.

WORKING TOGETHER

Maintaining organizational relationships requires you to navigate changes in leadership. Make sure that you are on familiar terms with more than one person in an organization or office. If the leadership is fragmented, pay special attention to and familiarize yourself with the general membership. The last thing you want is to have to trash the hard work you have done because an allied organization has had a shift in leadership in the middle of your campaign. Making sure that everyone is on board will ensure that your alliances are grounded in organizational commitments, not individual agreements.

Of course, part of maintaining these relationships means staying out of another group's organizational or political conflicts. If a leadership struggle or a nasty election is going on and people are taking sides, tread lightly and act professionally. If you are not a member of the organization, it is none of your business. In political conflicts, keep in mind that you need everyone to be an ally.

Strong relationships need to be maintained! Don't forget to keep your allies in the loop. Of course, you should include them in e-mail blasts and event invitations. Take the time to pick up the phone or drop into a meeting as well. If there's a lull in your campaign, be sure to drop a note to the group's leader and let him or her know that you'll be in touch when things pick up. Proper care and feeding will ensure that your organizational relationships don't wither on the vine.

USING WEB 2.0 TO FACILITATE GROUP COMMUNICATION

Along with using social networking for outreach and marketing purposes, you can also use it to facilitate communications among your supporters. Social-networking tools provide quick and efficient ways to communicate with large groups and to target smaller, curated groups at the same time. When organizing an advocacy campaign in addition to working your day job, these tools can save a lot of time and phone calls.

You can also use these tools to rally the troops. In January 2011, the Nielsen research company found that the average Facebook user spent almost seven and a half hours on Facebook each month.[1] If your group members are on the site, and they probably are, you may as well use it as a communication tool. Discussion groups, messaging, and chat capabilities are perfect for your purposes.

If your organization is set up on Facebook, you should be able to send group messages. You can easily send out mass announcements and reminders that you don't want cluttering up your page. Online discussion groups are sort of old school, but they can still be effective. Use them to test out new ideas with your members and to build consensus when making decisions.

TRADITIONAL WEB 2.0 PRODUCTIVITY TOOLS

There many online tools available that can help facilitate working in a group. Don't pass a draft of a press release around as an e-mail attachment. Upload it to a cloud service so that more than one person can work on it at once. Services that provide group access to documents include Dropbox, Evernote, and Google Docs (disclosure: we wrote this book in Google Docs!). Most of these services also offer smartphone applications that let you view and edit documents from anywhere. The documents you create can be embedded in a website or linked to via Facebook or any other social-networking site. Use tools to make lists and schedules for protests; use them to create press releases, lay out budget situations in an understandable way, edit blog posts in a group, and so on. Shared calendars provide an easy way to keep large groups of people apprised of events and meeting times. They can be embedded on websites and programmed to send reminders to participants. People are so busy and inundated with information that e-mail reminders are pretty much essential to ensure participation at events.

Although using social networking for group communication is fast and easy, you can't ignore those people in your organization who have opted out of the social-networking scene. Use e-mail to reach out to these people in a meaningful way and strengthen your group. Who knows, they may be amazing organizers.

We've mentioned it before, but your group needs to set up and use an organizational e-mail address for official group correspondence. Make absolutely sure that there is a responsible volunteer checking the inbox at least daily, more when during budget season. It can also be helpful to have e-mails sent to his or her phone. The volunteer who checks and responds to the e-mail should know about all group events and meetings, have access to all press releases and announcements, and be trusted to always be on message. If several people take on this duty, they must all be clear about who has done what and what has been dealt with and what hasn't. Missing e-mails is bad. Responding to e-mails with slightly different answers isn't all that great either.

USING E-MAIL MARKETING SERVICES FOR ORGANIZATION

Regular e-mail accounts can certainly be used for organization, but if you want something pretty and trackable, e-mail marketing services are the way to go. E-mail marketing services allow you to track how many e-mails are opened, how many bounce back and from whom, and which links have been clicked and how many times. You can glean a great deal of information from these services, including the kind of events your membership is interested in and whether they are getting sick of your e-mails.

One handy feature these services offer is the ability to set up multiple lists for different purposes. This allows the user to set up a list for volunteers, one for events, one for organizers, and so on. In this way you can target your e-mails to be more effective and avoid overloading peripheral people with information they don't want.

DEALING WITH DIFFICULT PEOPLE

Putting yourself out there and doing all this stuff is exhilarating and exhausting. You will meet people who think you are a hero, and you will deal with people who are certain that you are an idiot. Unfortunately, the people who see you as heroic tend to keep it to themselves, and the people who can't stand you will crow from the rooftops.

It's OK if people tell you that you are wrong. It's OK if they focus on your mistakes. It's OK if they refuse to see successes. Let it all roll off. Everyone has a right to an opinion. Some members of the library community (both professionals and users) love to share their entitled opinions with anyone who will sit still and listen. Let them talk: they may have some good ideas. Ask them to get involved, to contribute to your effort. It's a lot more fun to make a creative sign or write a snappy press release than it is to moan in your drink about what's gone wrong. If they continue to dwell on the negative and can't or won't get involved, then move on. Thank them for their time (because you always have to do that), then get back out there. Sure, this is easier said than done, but you have to let the baby cry for her candy. Let them tell you how you went astray last week while you stay focused on the changes you are going to make tomorrow.

NEUTRALIZE AND CO-OPT YOUR OPPONENTS

Unbelievable as it may seem, not everyone is going to agree with you. Although there aren't a lot of people who are vocally anti-library or who openly oppose the library's mission, there are a lot of folks whose spending priorities are focused elsewhere. When government's budgets tighten and resources are limited, competition can be fierce for what little there is to share.

Try to avoid going up against the so-called siren services; police and fire departments, basic safety services, will always trump libraries. Suggesting that cops should be fired or firehouses closed so the library can avoid layoffs will end up losing you backers. You might have an argument if the choice is between losing a branch library and buying a backup SWAT team wagon, but is it a worthwhile one? As always, choose your battles carefully (and these battles more carefully than most). Don't put yourself in a position in which people can conveniently see you as irrational or irrelevant.

Libraries don't exist in a vacuum, and neither do you. You can't make a case for your public library's budget by going against other public service providers. Budget cuts suck for everyone. Over the course of your campaign and during events, opponents, skeptics, and media types will probably try to pit you against other public service providers. Don't let them. Buying into the fake competition not only ensures that you lose valuable allies but also validates the notion that public service cuts are acceptable. Your job is to get out there and make an affirmative case for libraries, not to argue that a hundred library workers are more valuable than a hundred firefighters or a hundred teachers. Keep your events and message library focused. Cops and firefighters can actually be great allies. They understand camaraderie and the idea of working for something larger than oneself. Make it clear to them that you are not after their jobs. You may not march arm in arm with them, but having the backing of these powerful services is a very good thing.

Of course, some people don't want any government spending to occur whatsoever. These people see a building full of books as just more government waste. It's tough to negotiate with them. If they come from a business background, appeal to the return on investment that libraries provide (and if you use the term *ROI* in casual conversation, their eyes will light up). Point out that libraries are very efficient government agencies that provide wide-ranging services for a relatively small expense. Speak to them about the technical benefits the library provides and the resources it has for entrepreneurs and small business owners, who directly benefit the local business community. Don't forget to invoke Carnegie!

You must also be prepared to address individuals who are convinced that libraries can be staffed entirely by volunteers. The trick here is to frame the work as a trade, not a hobby. Would these people want to work a nine-to-five shift every Tuesday and Thursday, do storytime, or make a list of mysteries and romance novels coming out next month and prep it for ordering?

Not everyone can be persuaded, but don't avoid conflict. Activism is all about changing people's minds; if everybody agreed with you at the outset, there would be no need for a grassroots movement. Sometimes people opposing you just don't know enough or have no idea what the argument is really about. If you give them some facts, they may be able to see things another way. You will never bring all of them around to your point of view, but that doesn't mean you shouldn't constantly try.

NOTE

1. "January 2011 Top U.S. Web Brands and New Sites," Nielsenwire, February 11, 2011, http://blog.nielsen.com/nielsenwire/online_mobile/january-2011-top-u-s-web-brands -and-news-sites/.

4
PUTTING YOURSELF OUT THERE
THE NUTS AND BOLTS OF ADVOCACY

Getting active is great. It can be really fun to pull off events. They gel up your organization and they motivate people to get out and keep them coming back. They help you to get in the press, and they allow you to frame the debate the way you want it to be seen. Having an event, a rally, a march, or a read-in gets to the heart of activism and advocacy. Mobilizing people, bringing them together, and getting them moving toward something together is an incredible achievement in whatever form you can accomplish it.

Take time to think about your larger goals before you go rushing off to organize an event. What do you want out of it? Is this an attempt to get some press? Are you trying to collect massive amounts of petition signatures and postcards? Is there a meeting of politicians and decision makers whom you want to show your numbers to at a public hearing?

If you are trying for lots of petition signatures, then go where the foot traffic is, even if that is not near your library. If you are trying to get the press to come out, then make sure there is some kind of hook that will get them there. Are you trying to rally your supporters in the community? If so, don't plan an event at 10 a.m. on a workday. Think about what you want at the end of the whole thing, and create the event to fit those goals, not the other way around.

If you want a big press event, you need to be creative. "Librarians Protest Budget Cuts" is old news. "Librarians Read for 24 Hours" or "Zombie Librarians March to Protect City's Brains" have more zing and can get reporters excited about what you are doing. Give supporters and politicians something new, a fresh angle, and they will (hopefully) show up in force and get you in the media stream.

Are you trying to put pressure on politicians directly? Show up when they meet to talk about this stuff. Budget hearings are part of the process, so find out where and when they take place and see if you can give testimony. When you speak, be polite but firm, dress professionally, and have your talking points lined up and practiced in advance. Weep if necessary. Ideally, you want to get a bunch of your friends and supporters to come along with you and do the same thing.

Avoid pointless events. It can feel great to hold an angry sign and yell at the world (we certainly know it can), but if nobody is listening, you need to find another way to get your message out. Find people who are sympathetic, and find things to occupy their time with while they are out there supporting you. Soaking up the rays wearing a library T-shirt does not equal activism (sorry). Use the time and resources you have at hand. A dozen marchers protesting where neither politicians nor press can see them may seem like a waste of time, but if they are drawing a crowd or making a spectacle, they could be getting a huge number of petitions or postcards signed. Identify your target audience, and plan your event accordingly.

In every case, plan ahead. If you are thinking tactically, you will be able to use your time, personnel, and resources to best effect. Don't go to the budget hearing and scream while you throw books, don't have your beloved school librarian burn the mayor in effigy. (Rule of thumb: don't burn anybody in effigy; you end up looking like an idiot. We have debated burning books to protest budget cuts, but again, we are sticking to the not-crossing-the-burning-stuff line ourselves.) This is not to say that the same campaign cannot have a sweet lady (or gent) bring the tears to the politicians' eyes and have a radical street-theater event with puppets and balloon banners. Changing your tone keeps people on their toes and prevents them from putting you and your ideas in a box.

TONE

Remember that you get to set the tone for your event. We tend to try to keep things fairly chipper and fun, even when we are carrying a casket with a zombie librarian in it. Everyone has a lot on their plates. If your event promises to be compelling, fun, and rewarding, people will make time for you in their busy, busy lives and show up in droves.

It's not enough to merely set the tone. Give people something to do. People like to be involved. Of course, you don't want to make it onerous, but letting folks do some work allows them to feel useful and helps you out in turn. Have them fill out a postcard to the city council asking council members to restore the library budget (see the section "Letters and Postcards" later in this chapter). If they seem invested in that, then ask them to ask other people to fill out some postcards too. Is one of these people a mom with kids who just stopped for a minute but uses the library all the time? Maybe she would like to have her children color a ready-made "I Love My Library" coloring sheet that you have handy. Don't ask them to sweat too much, but don't ask them to sit there like dummies either. Just holding a sign gets pretty boring pretty quickly. Let people take a shift at the petition table, or the sign station, or working the crowd with a stack of postcards. Make things different, change tasks up, and people will stick around and probably find new ways to help out that you hadn't even anticipated.

It is incredibly important to reach out to the other public-service providers who are fighting cuts and to invite them to your events. By doing this, you concretely demonstrate that you consider them allies. Having a rally at your library branch? Make sure to drop off a flyer at your local firehouse and police precinct. Take the time to attend the events of other groups. A rally protesting education cuts is a great place to pass out flyers for your candlelight vigil and to make organizational connections. Show through your actions that the fight to protect public libraries is a fight to protect essential public services, period.

Actively solicit allies and supporters, but avoid guilt-tripping at all costs. "Being involved" means different things for different people. Some folks may feel comfortable attending a rally, but others may limit their involvement to gathering petition signatures or writing a letter to the editor. Whatever their comfort level, it is essential that people feel welcomed, and not shamed, to contribute as they feel appropriate. Ideally, supporters will dip their toes into the advocacy water, and slowly submerge themselves until they are full-fledged activists. This can't happen if they meet with derision or judgment over their initial level of activity. Many groups rightfully lose supporters early on because burned-out organizers guilt-trip and berate new recruits for not being "committed enough." Don't make that mistake. Remember to thank people for just showing up. Welcome the level of support you receive, and give people outlets to get more involved, but don't take it personally and lash out if folks don't act the way you want them to. You will be more successful in retaining increasingly active participants in the long run if you offer a friendly, welcoming, and supportive environment.

Guilt is a lousy motivator. Tell people, "You weren't there last time but you better be there this time," and you can rest assured they will never come out to an event again. Give people a purpose instead. "If you do" is very different from "because you didn't." Telling people that their involvement will make a difference will give them a reason to feel like they are a part of something.

ESSENTIALS

While planning a rally, march, or demonstration, it is imperative that you take the time to research local laws or ordinances relating to public gatherings. You have a legal right to assembly and free speech, but how those rights are expressed may be subject to regulation in your town. Many cities and towns restrict the location or size of gatherings, require permits, and ban the use of certain signs or props. Don't wait until the actual event to discover this. People who get their rally shut down because they didn't take the time to file the paperwork are not romantic martyrs to the cause; they are idiots who wasted the time of people who believed in them. You want to keep your participants safe and informed of any potential risks. If you have a National Lawyers Guild in your area, contact them. Ask your friendly and free public reference librarian to help you research local laws. Make sure to verify your findings with a reliable source, that is, the actual printed ordinance. Don't rely on hearsay of what is and isn't allowed: there is a big difference between what someone may find objectionable and what is actually illegal. Know your rights.

As an organizer, you have a responsibility to your participants. Are you billing an event as child-friendly? That may not be the best time to conduct civil disobedience. Ditto for events that you think will have a significant police presence. Be aware and considerate of the relationship between law enforcement and the community in preparing for events. This doesn't mean that you shouldn't protest, or march, or choose to engage in civil disobedience as tactics in your campaign. Just keep in mind that intents and aims should be clearly communicated with other participants so that they can make an informed decision to be there.

Library staff can be incredible activists, but they will not be your only activists, so remember to keep your membership open to anyone who is willing to speak up for the library. Ideally, both patrons and staff should be involved. People who use the library often like to help the library, and they will do this in varying ways as their lives permit. Make it as easy as possible for them to help out, and you will find it easy to get them on board. Remember that when patrons are involved in your efforts, they are probably out there in the community telling their friends and family about what you are doing, even when they are not out at rallies or petition drives. These connections with patrons go both ways and help make people feel a sense of ownership and connection to your cause and the library itself.

Open your group to everyone, and let all kinds of people participate in your grand struggle. A lot of library users would secretly love to be behind the desk. Let them feel that they are part of the club. Allow them to participate in significant ways, and they will make significant contributions. When possible, play to people's strengths. If the local university writer-in-residence is on your side, it is fine if he or she is only comfortable holding a sign, but you can at least *ask* that writer to write a letter to the editor, and/or a press release, and/or a poem, and/or a ballad if it looks like doing so would help your cause. Give people a chance to give you the best they've got, and you will be amazed by what you get in return.

If you've established that it is indeed OK for staff to engage in advocacy and activism, you will most likely find them a very motivated group. A quick reminder, though: whatever job distinctions there may be at work don't carry over to activism. If a custodian is a rally dynamo and your head of reference bobbles for a half hour at the petition table, it is pretty clear who you need to ask to take the lead on the ground at the next event. Find something else that needs to be done that plays to the strengths of your head of reference.

Library workers have a number of existing alliances that can successfully carry over into your campaign. Many libraries have at least some members in unions. These should be automatic contacts when you start reaching out to other groups. Various library professional organizations provide local networks of potential supporters motivated by a belief in libraries and an interest in the institution. They often do not have conflicts of interests as employees of the institution being advocated for and often bring in different circles of support, like the legal or academic communities. Contact the local chapters of every library association you can find. Ask them to forward your calls for support and rally invites to their e-mail lists, blogs, and websites. Make sure to ask them for an organizational endorsement. This is generally pretty easy for them (they want to support libraries, too) and gives your burgeoning organization credibility. Save NYC Libraries got the endorsement of about ten library organizations around the city, and each one made it easier to get the next. Saying that we had the backing of so many groups made our cause sound enormous even when we were just starting out. Their e-mail lists brought in some great supporters from the academic, business, law, and special library communities.

Let partner organizations mobilize and deliver their members. If they are really invested, then clearly label them in your event literature as sponsoring organizations, and consider letting them have a table at the event itself. Bring leaders in as contributors.

It may be hard to relinquish your group's control over an event, especially if you have been organizing it since the inception, but part of being a good leader is letting other people step up and have a prominent role as well.

You will have a lot of fledgling activists on your hands. You may be one yourself. Lots of people who turn up at your rallies may have never done this kind of thing before. You yourself may never have been to a "protest" of any kind in your life. Everyone has to start someplace, and you have a big role in determining what kind of experience it will be for them. Try to make it friendly and welcoming. Nobody wants to bring

---

DISRUPTIONS

If people are disrupting your event, you need to step up and do something about it. You have the option to engage, isolate, or neutralize them. If they are threatening or intoxicated, get the attention of your friendly law enforcement presence, and if law enforcement is not around, then make your own efforts to remove the disruptions. After all, protests are a lot like libraries. There are usually no problems, but you prepare so that you are not surprised if they come up. This does not mean bring pepper spray; it does mean having people around who are used to dealing with disruptive people and keeping them aware of any problems that arise so that a situation doesn't spiral out of control.

---

their kids to an environment that seems chaotic or tense. Keep things moving along a schedule and nice and calm, even if you yourself are anything but.

Keep people laughing and keep it fun. We don't really do candlelight vigils; we do read-ins instead. Vigils feel like they are awaiting death or reprieve, whereas read-ins are active stands against injustice. That difference in tone goes out to other events as well. We did a zombie march with a hearse and a casket and the whole deal, but we went with a zombie protest march against an impending brains recession rather than a funeral procession for the library. This is not to say that we will *never* have a vigil. We've discussed stuff as far out as hunger strikes, but that is all so depressing. Why make people sad when they are helping you out? Admittedly, our political context has so far not warranted taking an exclusively somber tone, but there were many points along the way during which we considered that approach and discarded it in favor of a breezier touch. Keep it light, keep it fun, and keep it safe, and people will keep coming back and supporting you.

Activism should be fun. It should be easy to engage in. Most of all, to actually command loyalty to a cause, it should be relevant to people's lives in a direct way. If no one's getting on board with an event or a campaign, maybe your group should review its approach. You may be providing easy steps to get involved, but your tone may be overbearing or your message too abstract. Don't be afraid to abandon your approach and start over again. As we said earlier, being involved means different things to different people. Don't be protest police—let people run with it and have some fun.

EVENTS

Even if you don't have a lot of (or any) money or a lot of people, you can still put on great events if you use your imagination and ingenuity. If you have a little money but no people, try something flashy, plug the hell out of it, and hopefully the people will follow. If you have a lot of people but no money, then let many hands lighten the load and do something that emphasizes how many bodies you can get out even if you don't have a dime for T-shirts. Play to your strengths when you are planning, and roll with the punches when things don't work out the way you exactly planned.

PROTESTS

These are pretty much what you picture when you imagine activism events. A bunch of you stand around waving signs and chanting slogans. There are a lot of variations on this, though, and lots of other events listed here are types of protests. The classic protest for its own sake can be hard to get people to show up to, so we suggest incorporating a narrative when you have an event. Do something with all those people. Hand over hundreds of petitions or postcards, read out loud, give away books, have a reason for being there other than that you are ticked off. Give the politicians and press something to see other than a bunch of angry people.

There are some important basic procedures to follow for any public rally. Get your permits and permissions. If you cannot assemble at a given site, find one adjacent that is friendly. If this is impossible, find one with symbolic import that will encourage assembly. Make sure you have contact with law enforcement and with relevant parks, municipal, or private security and custodial staff. Make sure everyone knows when the event is starting and stopping and exactly where the event is taking place and what the boundaries are. Write out a schedule, and for particularly complex events consider having site schematics, location managers, and even radio communication among key personnel. Have a small first-aid kit on hand, bring spare sunscreen, and have a spare tarp (just because they are really handy). Whatever form your event or "protest" takes, planning ahead will save you massive amounts of trouble at the event itself.

SOME PROTEST IDEAS

- Read-in
- Silent read-in
- Mass checkout
- Petition handover
- Postcard drop

- Children's rally
- Mobile library brigade
- Storytime sit-in
- Vigil
- Pink-slip burning

- Library hug
- Library sleep-in
- Any combination of the above

When you have come up with something new (and you will), let us know about it. Let *everybody* know about it.

MARCHES

Marches are moving protests. The logistics are more difficult, and clear communication with local authorities is much more important. Have your route clearly laid out, and make sure everyone gets a copy of it. If your crowd is spread out over a long route or is doing a walkathon, leave crew at key positions to point the way and cheer the marchers on. Be absolutely sure that you have traveled the route and have noted every instance in which you could potentially affect local businesses of residences. Do you block any driveways or service entrances? Are there choke points or blind corners? Will you be entering any already-crowded situations (e.g., the Brooklyn Bridge walkway on a lovely Sunday afternoon). None of these are deal breakers so long as you work things out in advance. Never block access to businesses. Messing with people's livelihoods makes you no friends, but being very visibly concerned with *not* messing with their trade can make you some very good friends who may use their business influence to your benefit. Keep things moving. Have provisions and plans in place for little kids and elders who may need a break along the route. Bring all the water you can lay your hands on, and if it is a long route, have water stations set up along the way. Pack extra Band-Aids and sympathy for blisters, and be sure to bring all the energy you've got.

PARTIES

Everyone loves a party. Planning them, however, is just as complicated as planning any other event. Figure out what you want from the party ahead of time. Is it a networking or social event? Is it to raise the profile of the library or of librarians in general? Are you trying to raise money? Parties can be great fund-raisers, but you must be sure that they are not going to cost you more to throw then you can hope to raise. Often, parties mean booze—they don't have to, but they often do. Generally, people don't get too schnockered at library events (generally), but be sensible and keep things in hand. Get a venue to take care of the booze, and they can shut off the drunk librarians.

Work with a place you know. Bars and coffeehouses are go-to meeting spots for causes and movements. If there is a place where you have been hatching plans (other than around your kitchen table), then talk to the owner. Is there a microbrewery or local distillery of any kind? See if they will donate a keg or case to your cause, and work out a split with the owners. Make sure that you are super grateful and complimentary of the venue, but remember that you are bringing people in, so don't let them treat you like a total patsy.

There are tons of fun ways to make money at parties. Solicit local businesses for prizes and then raffle them off. Sell T-shirts. Sell buttons. Sell desserts and candy. Sell whatever you can. Some supporters of ours suggested a kiss-a-librarian booth (full disclosure, it was actually "french a librarian"). While we applaud their eye for revenue potential, we question their motives.

CONCERTS

Do you have friends who are in a band? Do you have lots of friends in lots of bands? Can you find a venue that will give you 15–20 percent of the gate? Throw a concert, man—if you get a good gate percentage. The trick, of course, is to get as much of the money at the back end as you can while getting as much on the front end for free as you can. If you only get 10 percent of the gate, but half the musicians need to be paid something, and all the bands and their crews expect you to buy their brew, then you will end up owing the venue money on the bar tab.

Do you have access to a non-drinking-related space like a hall? Throw a variety show, and work out a split on the entrance fees with the venue. These can be really fun. With a mixture of acts there is usually something for everyone, and your performers have it a lot easier than trying to pull off an hour-long show on their own. Get a classical quartet, have them followed by a belly dancer, throw in some bluegrass, do a Shakespeare duet, bring on a juggler, and close with a power trio of faculty from the music department of the local university, and folks, you have one heck of a show. It goes without saying that a concert or show involves an incredible amount of very detailed planning. If you don't

---

NEUTRALIZING NUT JOBS

When you put yourself out there and try to attract attention to your cause, you will inevitably get some attention that you do not want. If you work in a library already, you have probably encountered people from the margins of society. Not transients, mind you, just folks who perhaps dance to a slightly different melody from most. These people will come to your rallies. Once at your rally they might ask you to a clandestine meeting so they can share secret government information, disseminate literature for a completely different cause that you do not agree with, or verbally assault you while you are made up as a clown. Don't laugh—every single one of those instances actually has happened to the authors of this book.

Deal with these people the way you deal with people who have a meltdown in the library. Try to be detached yet firm. If they are being disruptive, tell them that you would like to hear their views in greater detail and move them away from the crowd. If they resort to name-calling, introduce yourself (first name only), and offer to shake their hand. It is harder for people to marginalize you if they know your name. Introducing yourself and shaking hands can reset the social breaker and let you have a conversation instead of a shouting match.

None of these this may work, but fortunately, if you hang around public libraries, nut jobs are probably old news. Stay calm and collected, and don't get lured into anyone's game. Keep your temper and your dignity to yourself, and you will be fine. Let whatever they have to say roll off like rain. If you ignore them, isolate them, and refuse to fuel their fire, then their ire will burn out and they will wander off. If you are wondering how our adventures worked out, we did attempt the rendezvous but brought friends; we asked the pamphleteer to get his own rally, but when he refused we had someone follow him around and make counterarguments to his case anytime he stopped someone; and finally we asked the screamer if he realized that he was, in fact, yelling at a clown. Nut jobs neutralized!

have any experience with this kind of thing, reach out to the local theater for suggestions and assistance. Make sure that these events are scheduled down to the minute.

TOWN MEETINGS

As an activist, you should be a constant presence at town meetings. These events can take a lot of forms. You can attend your community's regular town meetings and state your case before the public directly. Many politicians have begun using the town meeting as a way to interact with voters. Consider attending these and stating your case or asking local politicians for clarity on their positions. Bear in mind that political meetings can get heated, so make the extra effort to always be scrupulously polite. Make your point and represent your cause. Don't look for trouble.

You can always throw your own town-hall meeting. Invite the public to come out and have a conversation about the library. Let them ask questions and offer opinions. If you work in libraries, you probably get a lot of both of those already. Getting a dialogue going is a great way to bring opponents around and to bring fresh allies to your side.

SPEAKING ENGAGEMENTS

Local groups like the Lions or Rotary are always on the lookout for outside speakers for their meetings. If you can get on their dance card, this is an amazing way to put your cause and issues before a group of people already invested in community service. These crowds don't want your hottest rhetoric, and being a firebrand in front of them will alienate more allies than it will recruit. They will, however, respond to discussions of what the library can (and does) do for its community. Let them know what could happen in both a best and a worst case. Let them know what you have planned for events. Make the case that the library is good for business and workforce development. Tell them about successful entrepreneurs who have used the library when they were starting out. Talk about teens who volunteered at the library and are now at or heading to top schools. This should be a pretty formal and staid presentation. Members of these groups are often heavily involved in local government and business communities. If you can influence these influencers, then this short speech and round of hand shaking can make a huge impact for your cause.

LETTERS AND POSTCARDS

Mail is a great way to get people's attention. Postcards, letters, and petitions have real physical weight. They are a tried-and-true activism tactic that has gotten only more powerful in the age of electronic activism. If politicians receive an electronic petition with a thousand signatures, they can still discount it with a click. Half that number of signatures spread over a hundred pages of paper is harder to blow off. Postcards are a great option. They can be printed pretty cheaply, and each signature has its own extra weight.

It can be tough to decide whom to send this mail to. One approach is to have a collection point at which all of your cards or petitions are assembled by a politician ally who then presents them on your behalf. The advantage here is that your ally will hold them and present them to his or her colleagues, hopefully to best effect. Another option is to present them en masse to a political body yourself. If you hand them off to any party who is not entirely friendly to your cause, ensure that there is a press presence to witness. The worst possible case is that the cards and letters go into a black hole. Don't send one or two at a time to people who may not agree with you. They could disappear and have no impact. Instead, make a situation in which you can present someone with hundreds of cards and stacks of petitions. That kind of weight makes your cause impossible to ignore.

The very first Urban Librarians Unite action was a postcard campaign, publicized and coordinated online using Web 2.0 tools. The idea was to find a way to meld online "clicktivism" with something that would generate real weight. What if, instead of a "like" on Facebook or a signature on a petition, we got people to fill out their own postcards? Each signature would then have individual substance. The first few hundred postcards were picked up for five cents each near the Empire State Building. After that, we asked groups to join us by purchasing custom postcards for the campaign (Local 1321, Queens Library Guild, sponsored the first print run). All of the postcards were preaddressed and delivered to a city council member, to aggregate their effectiveness. We joked for, hoped for, and have yet to get the final scene in the courtroom at the end of *A Miracle on 34th Street*, but we are still working on it.

Be creative with a letters-to-the-editor campaign. Avoid boilerplate lettering. Mass produced letters are transparent to editors, will probably not get published, and can alienate some newspaper staff. Provide your people with a framework, some cogent facts to cite, ideal outcomes, and invite them to add their own anecdotes. These elements combined make for good, and personal, letters to the editor. Recruit notable figures in your community and ask them to write on your behalf. Make this easy for them if they are not writers by having a prewritten letter that they can add to or edit if they choose. Ask the beloved retired principal to write on behalf of storytime. Is there a writer or minor celebrity in town? Odds are that they already use the library, so see if they will help you out. Could you get a number of educators, religious officials, business leaders, or artists to send a cosigned letter to the press? If you make your letters to the editor genuine, varied, and personal, then papers will pick them up and people will react to them.

STREET ART AND THEATER

You can use elements of street art (e.g., stickers, chalk) and political theater (e.g., puppets, costumes) as campaign tools. This kind of creative activism has incredible potential for libraries. Take your creative protests to the extreme. Build a huge librarian puppet eight feet tall and have it at all your rallies. Make yourselves up as zombies. Have on-the-spot librarians at political rallies and hearings. Spray-paint a decommissioned book truck white and fill it full of spray-painted ghost books to act as a ghostly reminder of services and collections lost. Change the story. Build an unusual and fresh narrative, and you will get people's attention. The important thing is to get your message in there in the blink of an eye when your librarian superhero costume has people's attention. The spectacle facilitates your message, not the other way around. If you are walking around on stilts wearing a clown wig, make sure everyone knows *why* you are walking on stilts wearing a clown wig.

STREET THEATER RESOURCES

Creative Direct Action Visuals Manual, by the Ruckus Society—this is an amazing assortment of resources to help you make really dynamic visuals for your events: http://ruckus.org/downloads/RS_ActionVisuals.pdf

68 Ways to Make Really Big Puppets, by Sara Peattie—you can buy this directly from Bread and Puppet, a huge political puppet group in Vermont: http://breadandpuppet.org

---

POSTMORTEMS AND FRAMING

After an event or campaign is over, it is incredibly tempting to relax and congratulate yourself for a job well done. Absolutely give into that instinct (activists who take care of themselves can stick it out for the long haul), but after you've gotten some sleep and the glow of accomplishment has subsided, take the time to conduct a postmortem. What tactics were more effective than others? What messages never connected with people? What event particularly resonated with your target audience? What argument was repeated over and over in every article and interview?

Reflection and assessment are crucial for your organization to separate the good ideas from the mediocre, the successful tactics from the fruitless, and the draining activities from the sustainable. Next time around, you will have the perspective that comes from experience and critique, and you can also save yourself some time and energy. Using criticism as a tool for organizational growth can happen only if you are receptive to criticism, and if you can offer it constructively in turn. You may feel territorial about an idea or protective of an event you organized, but ferreting out ways that you could have done it better is not an attack on you personally.

If your group received outside criticism over the course of the campaign, especially from someone working toward the same goal, this is the time to really assess whether there is any truth to the critique. This does not mean that you should take Internet trolls and random quacks seriously. If, however, there is a message that you're hearing repeatedly from folks, such as that your message is off or that the way you do things is alienating, it warrants examination.

Weathering criticism, small failures, and larger misfires of strategy are part and parcel of being an activist. Everyone out there working to build support and momentum toward a larger goal has experienced these and more. What is most important is how you deal with setbacks, how you take criticism, and how you develop your ability to bounce back and attack anew from another angle. Cultivating resilience will make you a better advocate for libraries and will be better for your mental health in the long run.

This means taking care of yourself. Commitment to a cause can easily obscure seemingly trivial things like getting a good night's sleep, eating regular meals, and having meaningful personal relationships with your loved ones. Don't make that mistake. You will not do anyone or "the cause" any favors if you're a miserable, exhausted, hungry shell of a person, and you will not be performing at your optimum potential. Cranky, stressed-out activists are also poor recruiters to the cause. They often do a pretty lousy job of convincing the public as well. Making activism fun means that you can have a healthy life and be a library warrior, too. Set the example!

Budget cuts aren't going away. Neither is the fight to defend public libraries, nor the need to continually articulate their value and importance. You are in this for the long haul, and therefore you need to think strategically and pace yourself. Building alliances, operating within a place of mutual respect, taking care of yourself, and paying attention to organizational and community dynamics are essential to building a movement that sustains itself beyond the annual campaign or efforts of a single person. Train for the marathon, not the sprint.

CONSTANT STATE OF ADVOCACY

Your budget season is over, so now what? You've put together an amazing group of people who all care deeply about libraries. You either got or didn't get what you wanted. What do you do with all of your momentum? It's much easier to start again in the next budget cycle if you already have a group and structure in place, so keep it going. If you saved your library in the current budget cycle, have a party and celebrate. Everyone probably worked very hard and deserves a break and recognition. If you want people to come back and help you next time, it's necessary to recognize their work. If you did not achieve your goals, it is even more important to be in touch with your supporters. They will look to you to find light in the darkness and help them understand what happened. If you "failed" this year, then you can use that as a springboard for next year, but you have to set that tone early before defeatism sets in. Find successes to celebrate, praise individual efforts, and start planning for the next round of the fight.

Clean up and archive your documents. If you are going to be doing similar events and letter-writing campaigns next year, there is no reason to start from scratch. Save your press releases and forms so that you have something to work with next time. At the same time, you may not need every single document you created during your campaign, and keeping the ones you don't need will make it difficult to find the ones that you do need next year, especially if you are using a file-sharing service. Take the time to weed out the half-finished documents and drafts, and label your files so you can hit the ground running.

Organize your contact's information. We get it—you were busy, and that's why it's all such a mess. Now that you aren't so busy, organize and label everything. Create lists of supporters, politicians, and media contacts. You will be thankful when you pull everything out next year to do it all over again. Send thank-you notes to people who particularly helped your cause like the politicians who went to the mat for you or the reporter who broke the story about your efforts. These reinforce important relationships and form bonds that you can build on for future activism efforts.

Don't let your website die! Advocacy is seasonal, so you won't always have the amount of content and traffic that you do in the midst of a budget fight, but that doesn't mean that you should let your website lie dormant. After you've posted your thank-you post, which you should do no matter what the outcome of your campaign was, think about linking to save the library campaigns in other towns, cities, and states. Not only should we support one another in the spirit of professionalism, but our campaigns can only benefit from the sharing of strategies, stories, and the countless defeats and successes that shape our work. Maybe you have some members or supporters who are interested in writing about library issues in general. Don't forget to check for dead links occasionally, as nothing says, "I've checked out" more than a bunch of links that don't go anywhere.

Ultimately, the best advocates for the library are the gifted and committed staff at the library itself. When people get great service, they value that service. When people can count on you for help when they need it, they will be much more likely to help you when you need it. Serve the public as if your life depended on it, and the life you save might be the institution itself. Communities value their libraries. Individuals love their libraries. Make your services, collections, and programs so great that even suggesting library cuts is political suicide.

As long as there are people out there who think that libraries are a luxury, we are going to have to keep talking about our services and success stories. The best advocacy tool is great customer service. Librarians shouting about funding is fast becoming normal. We need to go beyond that and build a movement that will take a stand against library budget cuts. Let's get serious! You are the fighters that can make this happen. Together we can make libraries safe for generations to come.

APPENDIX

 WEB Editable versions of the appendix materials are available at **www.alaeditions.org/webextras/.**

HUG THE LIBRARY

We **LOVE** the library—let's give it a snuggle!

**Saturday
June 4th
2pm**

Stephen A. Schwarzman Building
41st Street @ 5th Avenue

Love Your Library, Fight the Budget Cuts

More information at www.savenyclibraries.org

WE WILL NOT BE SHUSHED

A 24-HOUR READ-IN TO SUPPORT
NYC LIBRARIES

It' time to stand up for public libraries and say NO
to the budget cuts.
It's time to stand up and READ.

4pm Saturday June 11th – 4pm Sunday June 12th
Steps of the Brooklyn Public Library
@
Grand Army Plaza

More information and sign-ups at www.savenyclibraries.org

Elected Official Contact Tracker

Name/Position	District	Office Phone #	E-mail	Chief of Staff	Scheduler	Twitter

Media Contact Tracker

News Organization	Website	Phone #	Fax	Press Release	Media Blast

Volunteer Assignment Worksheet

For large events it can be helpful to create a volunteer schedule. This helps you make sure all of your tasks are covered. It can also help keep track of who is supposed to be doing what, something that frequently gets lost in larger rallies and events. You may need to create a more complicated schedule for larger events.

Breaking tasks up into time slots also gives volunteers some time to breathe and just "be at the event." Working at a rally is work, and volunteers need breaks so they don't burn out.

Volunteer Assignment Schedule			
Time	[Task #1]	[Task #2]	[Task #3]
1pm	John Smith		

Interview Cheat Sheet

Talking to the press can be stressful if you've never done it before. Use this cheat sheet to memorize your statistics and talking points. You can even have it sitting in front of you for radio interviews (no one can see it but you!).

The Numbers:

If you keep track of your statistics, and keep them in one place, you'll never have to scramble to answer a question. This is one of the most important parts of preparing for an interview.

Last Year's Budget	
Proposed Budget	
% Difference	
Service Hours	
Proposed Service Hours	
% Difference	

# of Proposed Layoffs	
Circulation	
Program Attendance	
Children's Program Attendance	
Gate Count	

Your Library's Story:

This is where you really get to say what the library means to your community. Numbers and statistics can tell part of the story, but it's so important to add a human side. It's good to be able to say, "We helped this many people get search for jobs last year." But it's so much better when you can say, "I helped this single mom find a job, and she didn't get evicted from her home, because of the library."

_____

_____

_____

_____

_____

_____

_____

_____

_____

_____

_____

Rally in a Box

We challenge everyone everywhere to empower themselves and hold their own library rally. Don't feel intimidated! It doesn't have to be huge. If one person stops and asks what's going on, that is a success! If ten people stop, then you have scored a victory and made an impact in the community that you serve.

5 Rules

- No trashing the mayor (we may all want to, but it doesn't do us any good)
- No trashing the library director (again, not gonna help)
- Don't obstruct anything (roads, entry to library, etc.)
- Don't work the rally on work time (ask your individual manager for suggestions)
- Bust your ass: either do the work and hit it hard, or step aside

5 Tools

- Facebook for communications
- Flyers to spread the word
- Talking points to keep you focused
- Checklist so you don't forget anything
- Camera so you can share it

5 Talking Points

- Libraries help small businesses and job-seekers
- Libraries are the community cultural storehouse
- Libraries are cost effective and preserve community households' savings
- Libraries help kids and teens
- Libraries are democratic—everyone benefits from them

5 Activities

- **Clasping hands around the library:** Get the whole crowd into it! Find anyone you can to help—HUG your library and keep it safe! Do it even if you don't have enough to surround it!
- **Children's rally:** Let the little ones take charge! Make it a munchkin rally with tiny signs, and get the bigger kids to be your readers.
- **Mini Read-In:** Put up a sign, open a book, start reading, invite your friends, repeat! We did ours for 24 hours but you can do an hour, two, four, or more.
- **Mini-March:** March around the exterior of the library - not just once, but for a set amount of time. Patrol the perimeter, be loud, be proud, hold up your signs and protect your library like soldiers on watch!
- **Library Art Quilt:** Create and display a children's art "quilt" of paper art stapled together. Get all the kids to create art in support of the library for a few days. Staple them all together and see (and photograph) how big a space it fills! Bring it outside and show the world how much you love your library!

5-Point Checklist

- **Get the OK:** Permission from library branch manager and if necessary, the library's government affairs office
- **Tell The World!:** Make flyers & post on bulletin boards and around neighborhood
- **Include your allies:** Notify Friends group & any potential supporting organizations or groups in the neighborhood (local schools, etc.)
- **Don't overlook the obvious:** TELL YOUR CUSTOMERS
- **Prep:** Have all of your supplies ready to go - petitions, camera, sunscreen (you don't want Lauren's trucker tan!), signs, t-shirts, buttons, talking points, paper megaphone (rolled up card stock), courage, friends ❤

Urban Librarians Unite
www.savenyclibraries.org
savenyclibraries@gmail.com

For Immediate Release

October 26, 2010

Media Contact: Lauren Comito 646.555.0100

Save NYC Libraries Postcard Campaign and Urban Librarians Unite Announce
Halloween Zombie Walk to Save NYC Public Libraries
October 31, 2010
11:00 a.m.–3:00 p.m.

Brooklyn, New York—October 2010—Urban Librarians Unite announce a Halloween Zombie Walk in support of New York City's public libraries, to be held October 31, 2010, beginning at Cadman Plaza, Brooklyn and continuing over the Brooklyn Bridge to commence at City Hall, New York, New York, USA. Official website: www.savenyclibraries.org.

The Halloween Zombie Walk brings library-loving New Yorkers together for a day of public theater to draw public attention to the mid-year budget cuts faced by New York City's public libraries. What does any of this have to do with zombies? Well, without libraries there are simply no brains, and zombies need to eat brains to live. With libraries across the city closed on weekends there is a desperate food shortage. So New York City's zombie librarians will be walking across the Brooklyn Bridge to City Hall this Halloween to protest the drastic cuts to their food supply. These zombies are starving and without the support of the public library their future appears grim.

New York City's three library systems serve 8 million residents from a combined 212 locations, numbering over 43 million visits in FY'09. Since the economic crisis began, library use has been at an all-time high, with many New Yorkers depending on their local library for access to the information, resources, and programs necessary to conduct job searches, complete their education, navigate the Internet, and access public services.

Mayor Bloomberg's projected mid-year budget adjustment will cut funding for libraries by $16.5 million—5.4% across the board. This comes on the heels of a devastating August reduction of $30 million that decimated weekend library service. Three years of brutal cuts during the biggest economic crisis in a generation have reduced public library funding by a shocking $74.5 million since 2008, or 20%. Additional cuts will result in further service reductions and layoffs, right before the holiday season. Unless Mayor Bloomberg and the City Council maintain funding, libraries' ability to provide New Yorkers with job search help, afterschool tutoring, computer access and instruction, English classes, and research assistance will be sharply reduced by December 2010.

Dress in your bookish zombie best and march/shamble your way to City Hall to support your local library and feed your brain.

For more information on the Halloween Zombie Walk, please contact savenyclibraries@gmail.com

###